The Upanishads

The Upanishads

A New Translation

Vernon Katz and Thomas Egenes

Jeremy P. Tarcher/Penguin
An imprint of Penguin Random House
New York

JEREMY P. TARCHER/PENGUIN
An imprint of Penguin Random House LLC
375 Hudson Street
New York, New York 10014

Library of Congress Cataloging-in-Publication Data

Upanishads. English.
The Upanishads / a new translation by Vernon Katz and Thomas Egenes.
p. cm.—(Tarcher cornerstone editions)
Includes bibliographical references.
ISBN 978-0-399-17423-0 (paperback)
I. Katz, Vernon, translator. II. Egenes, Thomas, translator. III. Title.
BL1124.54.E5 2015 2015002867
294.5'9218—dc23

Printed in the United States of America

BOOK DESIGN BY LAUREN KOLM

Penguin Random House

Contents

Preface

I first met the Upanishads in an upstairs room in All Souls College, Oxford. There were about eight of us seated around Dr. Radhakrishnan, who was then Sir Sarvepalli Radhakrishnan, Spalding Professor of Eastern Religions and Ethics at Oxford University. Here was this great man speaking to just a few people in his sitting room. His audience was equally divided between a few students and a few elderly ladies, mostly from North Oxford. This was the late nineteen forties, and widespread interest in Eastern religions and philosophy had to wait till the sixties. Dr. Radhakrishnan had founded the Group for the Study of Religions. I was its secretary, and we invited speakers from different religions. We were always on the point of folding.

We were lucky to be so few because we had more of Dr. Radhakrishnan's attention. We started with Robert Ernest Hume's translation of the short Īsha Upanishad. The Īsha Upanishad is the usual starting point for the study of the Upanishads—rather unfortunately, because to my mind it is one of the most difficult. However, though I could not fully understand it, I was hooked. As we read through more Upanishads, the conviction grew that here was the truth. It was self-evident. No proof was needed, even across the span of centuries. I had stumbled on it, and I have never wavered from this conviction. These fellows knew what they were talking about. They had seen through the veil.

It was quite clear: This was not about belief, it was about experience. The sages were speaking about states of consciousness in this life that could be experienced by anyone. The fundamental insight was that the deepest layer of one's own experience, one's Self, was identical with the basis of the world outside. There was a unity of all things.

Dr. Radhakrishnan saw it as his mission to bring the knowledge of Indian philosophy to the outside world and to protect it from misinterpretation. His particular *bête noire* was Albert Schweitzer, who accused Indian thought of world and life negation. Dr. Radhakrishnan made it his business to refute him with numerous quotations about engaged action.

Dr. Radhakrishnan did not set out to be a guru. He was a philosopher who, with a wonderful command of the English language, pointed the way to the truth that his students had then to find in their own lives. Later, I was fortunate to find a teacher in Maharishi Mahesh Yogi, who could lead me to the actual experience that Dr. Radhakrishnan spoke about. Even in the early days, the Upanishads were not completely theoretical for me. I found the sages' matter-of-fact utterances moving, much more so than devotional texts. They gave me a glow, but that is not the same as actually experiencing the state or states of consciousness of which the Upanishads speak. Maharishi opened the way through his simple teaching which, just because of its simplicity, posed no obstacles to inner experience. I was very fortunate to come into contact with these great teachers who opened up the wisdom of the Upanishads to me.

—Vernon Katz

Introduction

The word *upanishad* means "sit down near": *upa* (near), *ni* (down) and *shad* (sit). Traditionally, the student sat down near the teacher to receive secret instruction, and in this way knowledge was passed down from teacher to student, linking each new generation back to the ancient tradition of the Upanishads. Many of the Upanishads consist of a dialogue between teacher and student in the deep quietude of a forest hermitage (*āshrama*) or in the home of the teacher (where the students lived as part of a system called *guru-kula*).

The great teacher Shankara explained the word *upanishad* as "the knowledge of Brahman by which ignorance is destroyed."[1] In other accounts, "sit down near" (*upanishad*) refers to the hidden connection between everything, whether it is the connection between the teacher and student, or more broadly, the infinite correlation among all things, the oneness of reality. In this way the word *upanishad* might be thought of as a state of consciousness in which everything is connected to one's own Self.

According to India's ancient tradition of knowledge, the Upanishads were cognized by *ṛishi*s, or seers. The profound truths dawned spontaneously in the silent depths of their consciousness and were recorded by them and passed down through generations, first orally and later in written form.

According to the Muktikā Upanishad[2] there are 108 Upanishads, although scholars later recorded more than two hundred. The first ten are considered to be the principal Upanishads: Īsha, Kena, Katha, Prashna, Muṇdaka, Māṇdūkya, Taittirīya, Aitareya, Chāndogya and Bṛihadāraṇyaka. Sometimes the Shvetāshvatara is also added, bringing the list to eleven. Shankara commented on these eleven. Because he also referred to four other Upanishads (Kaushītakī, Jābāla, Mahānārāyaṇa and Paingala) in his commentary on the Brahma Sūtras, these Upanishads are sometimes also included as principal Upanishads, bringing the list to fifteen (or fourteen, if the Shvetāshvatara Upanishad is not included). Each of the Upanishads is associated with one of the four Vedas: Ṛik,[3] Sāma, Yajus[4] and Atharva. For the nine Upanishads in this volume, the Aitareya belongs to the Ṛig Veda; the Kena belongs to the Sāma Veda; the Katha, Taittirīya and Shvetāshvatara belong to the Kṛishṇa Yajur Veda (the Yajur Veda has two branches); the Īsha belongs to the Shukla Yajur Veda; and the Prashna, Muṇdaka and Māṇdūkya belong to the Atharva Veda. Upanishads of the same Veda often have the same introductory and concluding verse (*shānti-pātha*).

Some of the Upanishads are in verse, others are in prose and a few are a mixture of both.[5] While several Upanishads are short, such as the Māṇḍūkya (twelve verses) and the Īsha (eighteen verses), other Upanishads are considerably longer, such as the Bṛihadāraṇyaka and Chāndogya Upanishads.[6] Slight variations in wording are found, as they have been passed down in an oral tradition for thousands of years.[7]

The Upanishads are the last part or culmination of the Veda and so are called *Vedānta*. They are known as the *gyāna kāṇda*, the section of the Veda that deals with knowledge—knowledge of the ultimate reality. Since the Upanishads are part of the Veda, they are regarded as *shruti*, or "that which is heard." Traditionally, they are considered to be *apaurusheya*, which means they are not the creation of individuals, not made up like poetry; rather they were revealed to enlightened seers who saw and heard these truths in the depths of their awakened consciousness. The Upanishads are also thought to be *nitya*—true for all time, all places and all people.

Influence of the Upanishads

The Upanishads have enjoyed a growing global influence over the centuries. The first known translation of the Upanishads, from the original Sanskrit into Persian, was commissioned in 1656 by Muhammad Dara Shikoh, the eldest son of Shah Jehan, who built the Taj Mahal. In 1802, the French scholar Abraham Anquetil-Duperron translated the Persian volume into French and Latin. The German philosopher Arthur Schopenhauer read Anquetil-Duperron's Latin translation and famously said of the Upanishads:

The Upanishads are the production of the highest human wisdom and I consider them almost superhuman in conception. The study of the Upanishads has been a source of great inspiration and means of comfort to my soul. From every sentence of the Upanishads deep, original and sublime thoughts arise, and the whole is pervaded by a high and holy and earnest spirit. In the whole world there is no study so beneficial and so elevating as that of the Upanishads. The Upanishads have been the solace of my life and will be the solace of my death.[8]

Influenced by Schopenhauer, the German scholar Paul Deussen translated the Upanishads and said, "On the tree of wisdom there is no fairer flower than the Upanishads and no finer fruit than the Vedānta philosophy."[9]

In America, Henry David Thoreau, Ralph Waldo Emerson and Walt Whitman were among the first to read the literature of India. Thoreau described the universal nature of the Vedas and eloquently gave an account of reading them:

What extracts from the Vedas I have read fall on me like the light of a higher and purer luminary, which describes a loftier course through a purer stratum,—free from particulars, simple, universal. It rises on me like the full moon after the stars have come out, wading through some far summer stratum of the sky. . . . One wise sentence is worth the state of Massachusetts many times over.[10]

Emerson noted, also eloquently, how the ancient literature of India resolves many of the questions of existence that the modern mind is engaged in solving:

It was as if an empire spoke to us, nothing small or unworthy, but large, serene, consistent, the voice of an old intelligence, which in another age and climate had pondered and thus disposed of the questions that exercise us.[11]

Walt Whitman read the Upanishads and described the universal spirit of this knowledge:

These are the thoughts of all men in all ages and lands,
    they are not original with me,
If they are not yours as much as mine
    they are nothing or next to nothing,
If they do not enclose everything they are next to nothing,
If they are not the riddle and the untying of the riddle
    they are nothing,
If they are not just as close as they are distant
    they are nothing.[12]

The Austrian physicist Erwin Schrödinger discussed the universal nature of knowledge and the universal nature of consciousness found in the Upanishads:

There is no kind of framework within which we can find consciousness in the plural; this is simply something we construct because of the temporal plurality of individuals, but it is a false construction. . . . The only solution to this conflict insofar as any is available to us at all lies in the ancient wisdom of the Upanishad.[13]

Schrödinger's contemporary, the Danish physicist Niels Bohr, said, "I go into the Upanishads to ask questions."[14]

Referring to the Upanishads as "some of the most sacred words that have ever issued from the human mind," Rabindranath Tagore wrote, "The messages contained in these, like some eternal source of light, still illumine and vitalize the religious mind of India. . . . Seekers of life's fulfillment may make living use of the texts, but can never exhaust them of their freshness of meaning."[15]

One of the most influential persons to introduce the Upanishads to a wider Western audience was the Oxford scholar and second president of India, Sarvepalli Radhakrishnan. In 1953, while vice president of India, he published his translation of the Upanishads. Here he identifies their central theme:

> Anyone who reads the Upanishads in the original Sanskrit will be caught up and carried away by the elevation, the poetry, the compelling fascination of the many utterances through which they lay bare the secret and sacred relations of the human soul and the ultimate reality.[16]

Principal Themes in the Upanishads

The Upanishads are a celebration of the awakening of the Self (*Ātman*),[17] a state of unbounded pure being, pure bliss. They reveal the great truth of life: The Self of the individual is identical to the Self of the universe (*Brahman*). They sing out, "I am totality" (*ahaṁ brahmāsmi*).[18] The wholeness of life, Brahman, expresses itself as every particle of creation and as every human being. This is the profound message of the Upanishads.

The Self, Unbounded Awareness

As we have seen, the Upanishads define Ātman as the Self, the inner essence that transcends the personality. The Self is awareness itself, devoid of any content such as thoughts, feelings and perceptions. It is pure wakefulness, the awareness that enables one to be conscious. Like the silent depth of the ocean, the Self is described as the abstract core of the mental and physical levels of reality. It is not limited by any kind of physicality; it is pure spirituality, with no distinctions, no boundaries, no thoughts, no emotions, no sensations—just pure, unbounded awareness aware of itself.

While the Upanishads describe the Self as nonlocalized, they refer to the space within the heart as "the seat of consciousness," the place where consciousness is most vibrant, often referred to as a secret cave. For example, the Katha Upanishad says, "The inner Self is ever seated deep in the hearts of men,"[19] and the Muṇḍaka Upanishad describes the Self as set in the heart:

Vast, divine, of inconceivable form,
subtler than the subtle, that shines forth,
farther than the farthest, and yet here, near at hand.
It is here within those who see, set in the secret place of the heart.

Not by the eye is it grasped, nor even by speech,
nor by the other senses, nor by austerity or action.
When one's nature is purified by the clarity of knowledge,
only then, as he meditates, does he perceive him, the indivisible.[20]

In these verses, after first locating the Self in the region of the heart, the Upanishad discusses how the Self is known. The Self is not known through sight, because it has no form. Neither is the Self known through hearing, because it has no sound. The Self is known when the mind has completely settled and there are no perceptions of anything limited or temporal in nature. What remains is awareness itself in its unbounded state. One is still aware, but there is no localized object of awareness. Awareness is aware of itself alone, as described in the Bṛihadāraṇyaka Upanishad:

There he does not see. Though seeing,
he does not see. The seer does not cease seeing,
because he is indestructible. But there is no second,
nothing other than himself that
he could see.

There he does not speak. Though speaking,
he does not speak. The speaker does not cease speaking,
because he is indestructible.
But there is no second,
nothing other than himself to whom he could speak.

There he does not hear. Though hearing,
he does not hear. The hearer does not cease hearing,

because he is indestructible. But there is no second,
nothing other than himself that he could hear.

There he does not think. Though thinking,
he does not think. The thinker does not cease thinking,
because he is indestructible. But there is no second,
nothing other than himself about which he could think.

There he does not know. Though knowing,
he does not know. The knower does not cease knowing,
because he is indestructible. But there is no second,
nothing other than himself that he could know.[21]

Each of these verses describes awareness, but not awareness of anything in particular. There are no thoughts, no sounds, nothing to see, and yet one is awake. All objective experience has disappeared and only pure subjectivity remains. This is the experience of the Self, often described as "pure being." The Kena Upanishad refers to the Self as the "the ear of the ear, the mind of the mind, the speech of speech, the breath of the breath, the eye of the eye."[22] Pure consciousness is the knower, and all other values are the means through which it knows the subtle and gross aspects of manifest life.

Ātman is not only a theoretical concept, but a universal reality that the Upanishads advise the seeker to realize. In the Bṛihadāraṇyaka Upanishad, the famous teacher Yāgyavalkya, before departing to the forest, says in his last words to his wife Maitreyī, "That *Ātmā*[23] alone is worthy of seeing, hearing, contemplating and realizing."[24] This message from Yāgyavalkya is the heart of the Upanishads. The Brahma Sūtras, which are a clarification of the Upanishads, refer to this passage (*vishaya vākya*) in the first section (*adhikaraṇa*), indicating that the experience of the Self, unbounded pure consciousness, is the central teaching of the Upanishads.

Brahman, the Totality

If Ātman is like a wave in the ocean, the whole ocean is Brahman. The Muṇḍaka Upanishad describes the universal nature of Brahman:

Brahman, truly, is this immortal.
Brahman is in front, Brahman is behind,
it is to the right and to the left, it extends below and above.
This whole world is nothing but Brahman, the supreme.[25]

From the standpoint of the highest state of consciousness, everything is Brahman, which is why it is translated as "totality" or "wholeness." For example, the Chāndogya Upanishad says, "All this is totality" (*sarvaṁ khalvidaṁ brahma*),[26] meaning that Brahman exists within all things: Brahman is the ultimate content out of which everything and everyone in the cosmos is made. The Māṇḍūkya Upanishad says, "Truly, all this is Brahman" (*sarvaṁ hyetad brahma*).[27] A passage in the Īsha Upanishad describes Brahman:

It is one, unmoving, swifter than the mind.
The senses cannot reach it. It darts ahead.
Standing still, it outruns those who run.
Within it the breath of life supports all that stirs.

It moves and it moves not.
It is far away and it is close by.
It is within all this.
It is outside all this.[28]

Brahman is within all things and also transcends all things. Brahman is in this world and beyond this world.[29] Brahman is unmanifest and manifest, unity and diversity, silence and dynamism. It is the eternally self-aware wholeness that is more than the sum of its own innumerable aspects.

According to the Upanishads, the realization of Brahman (*brahma vidyā*) is the purpose of life. Like a compass that is always turned toward the north, the mind is always directed toward Brahman because Brahman is a state of happiness: "Brahman is that toward which the mind moves, as it were, that by which it is ever aware and that which forms its purpose."[30]

The Self Is Brahman

Because Brahman permeates every aspect of creation, it also permeates each of us. In other words, Brahman is our own being, our own pure consciousness. In this sense, Brahman is the same as Ātman. Brahman is the ocean and Ātman is a drop in the ocean. Each drop of water can say, "I am the ocean," because each drop is made of the same substance of which the ocean is made. The fully realized not only perceive the drop merging into the ocean but, as the Indian mystic poet Kabir writes, perceive the ocean merging into the drop.

The identity of Ātman with Brahman is the main principle of the Upanishads, expressed in the saying "Thou art that" (*tat tvam asi*).[31] This is one of four great expressions, called *mahāvākyas*, that were emphasized by Shankara in his commentaries on the Upanishads. In addition to "Thou art that," these expressions are: "I am totality" (*ahaṁ brahmāsmi*),[32] "This Self is Brahman" (*ayam ātmā brahma*)[33] and "Consciousness is Brahman" (*pragyānaṁ brahma*).[34] These celebrated expressions convey one common meaning: Brahman, which pervades everything, can be known within each individual. The full meaning of each mahāvākya is gained through direct experience: One can access the whole of creation just by accessing one's own Self.

The identification of Ātman with Brahman is found throughout the Upanishads. For example, the Taittirīya Upanishad states, "He who is here in the person and he who is there in the sun—he is one."[35] A passage from the Īsha Upanishad says, "He who is that person afar, I am he."[36] (The words *he* and *person* in the above quotes do not refer to Brahman as a limited individual entity, but as unbounded being.) The Kena Upanishad explains how one may have a tendency to venerate Brahman as far off, or as being limited to only this or that particular form, whereas Brahman is wholeness, a wholeness which includes the person who is doing the venerating:

That which is not uttered by speech,
but by which speech is spoken—
that alone know to be Brahman,
not what people venerate here.

That which is not thought by the mind,
but by which, they say, thought is thought—

that alone know to be Brahman,
not what people venerate here.

That which one does not see with the eye,
but by which the eye sees—
that alone know to be Brahman,
not what people venerate here.

That which is not heard by the ear,
but by which hearing is heard—
that alone know to be Brahman,
not what people venerate here.

That which is not breathed by breath,
but by which breath is breathed—
that alone know to be Brahman,
not what people venerate here.[37]

In the above verses, we see that the essential nature of Brahman is the transcendental reality that animates the senses, as well as the senses themselves.

The identification of the Self with Brahman is the great principle upon which the Upanishads stand. In other words, any individual point of creation, no matter how minuscule, contains the whole of creation, like a set of pearls in which each pearl contains the entire strand. In a similar way, the DNA of each cell contains the information for the entire physiology. The universe of the Upanishads is holographic: Each point of infinity is yet infinity, and infinity is made up of innumerable points. Brahman expresses itself as every aspect of creation, while ever remaining the limitless essence of all its manifestations. A passage from the Muṇḍaka Upanishad illustrates how Brahman serves as the ultimate content from which all life is woven:

His head is fire, his eyes are the moon and the sun,
his ears are the regions of space, his speech is the Vedas unfolded,
his breath is the wind, his heart is the universe,
and from his feet comes the earth.
Truly, he is the inner Self of all beings.[38]

He on whom are woven sky, earth and the space between,
also mind, along with all the vital organs—
know him alone as the one Self.[39]

Fulfillment of Desire

Desire provides a direction for consciousness to become materialized, and therefore life-supporting desires are the means through which life flows. Denial of desire through withdrawal is not the ideal found in the Upanishads, which portray the fulfillment of desire as a natural consequence of knowing the Self. For example, the Kena Upanishad points out that "Through the Self one gains strength" (*ātmanā vindate vīryam*). The Sanskrit word for strength is *vīryam,* which also means "vitality" or "energy."

In addition, the Taittirīya Upanishad describes the material benefits for one who knows the Self and has realized Brahman:

He becomes great in offspring and cattle,[40]
great in the radiance of Brahman.
He becomes great in fame.[41]

When the Self is realized through direct experience, the individual enjoys a state of contentment in which desires are no longer experienced as unfulfilled needs that cling to the heart. Then whatever the individual might require for the maintenance of life will be produced through the creative power of his or her own nature. The Muṇdaka Upanishad explains how desires are fulfilled in an effortless manner for one who knows the Self:

Whatever world a man of purified nature sees clearly
in his mind, and whatever desires he desires,
that world and those desires he wins.[42]

He who knows Brahman dwelling in the secret place,
in the field of the transcendent,
wins all desires together with Brahman, the all-knowing.[43]

The Katha Upanishad expresses the same idea:

This imperishable indeed is Brahman.
This imperishable indeed is the supreme.
For one who truly knows this imperishable,
whatever he desires is his.[44]

Transcending the Intellect

In the Upanishads, the Self is more than an intellectual concept—it is a living experience. For example, the Katha Upanishad declares, "This Self cannot be attained by instruction, nor by the intellect, nor yet by much learning."[45] The Bṛihadāraṇyaka Upanishad says, "Let him not ponder over words, for many words are weariness."[46] Since the Self transcends logic, the Katha Upanishad states that the Self must be learned from someone who knows it by direct experience:

Taught by an inferior man, this Self cannot be easily known,
even though often reflected upon. Unless taught by one
who knows him as none other than his own Self,
there is no way to him, for he is subtler than subtle,
beyond the range of reasoning.[47]

Here the Upanishad explains that the Self is known through direct experience of pure consciousness, not through mere learning. The Self is known on the level of pure being, which goes beyond the intellect: "When known through an awakening, it is rightly known."[48] The Upanishads are critical of knowledge obtained through scholarly study alone:

Living in the midst of ignorance,
wise in their own eyes, thinking themselves scholars,
fools go round and round, running here and there,
like the blind led by the blind.[49]

The Katha Upanishad points to the danger of trying to know the Self through the intellect alone: "Not by logic can this realization be won."[50] Logic involves fragmentation, a feature of the intellect, which discriminates. However, with the experience of universal being, a continuum of existence dominates awareness, and fragmentation is seen in the larger context of wholeness. The Katha Upanishad emphasizes the danger of attempting to know the Self solely through intellectual knowledge:

He who has not discarded wrong action,
who is not tranquil, who is not collected,
whose mind is not at peace,
cannot attain this Self through knowledge.[51]

The warmth of the sun, the smell of jasmine, the singing of birds—almost everything people love about life escapes the comprehension of the intellect, because direct enjoyment of anything at all is experienced as the flow of consciousness, which transcends intellectual analysis. According to the Upanishads, the ultimate experience of Brahman is a state of being that goes beyond words. A passage from the Taittirīya Upanishad describes how "words turn back" from the experience of Brahman:

From where, before reaching it,
words turn back, along with the mind—
he who knows the bliss of Brahman,
fears not at any time.[52]

Happiness

The Upanishads repeatedly state that reality is bliss, *ānanda.* Ānanda becomes enlivened by knowing the Self, because the essential nature of the Self is bliss, as this passage from the Taittirīya Upanishad states:

Surely by grasping the essence, one is filled with bliss.
Who indeed would breathe, who would be alive
if this bliss did not pervade space?
For this essence alone bestows delight.[53]

Bliss replaces anxiety. The Taittirīya Upanishad describes how a person rids himself from distressing thoughts as a result of experiencing bliss: "He does not torment himself, thinking, 'Why have I not done what is right? Why have I done what is sinful?' Knowing this [the bliss of Brahman], he frees himself from these thoughts."[54] Numerous passages in the Upanishads state that fear and guilt vanish for one who has realized the Self. For example, the Chāndogya Upanishad says, "Knowing the Self, one overcomes sorrows and suffering,"[55] and the Katha Upanishad says, "Having known the vast, all-pervading Self, the wise man does not grieve."[56] The Taittirīya Upanishad states, "One is freed from fear only when he finds that fearless ground—invisible, bodiless, unutterable, undefined."[57] The Muṇḍaka Upanishad says that the realization of Brahman takes a person beyond sorrow: "He passes beyond sorrow. He passes beyond evil. Freed from the knots of the heart, he becomes immortal."[58] The Katha Upanishad describes freedom from fear as a by-product of the experience of the Self:

He who knows this enjoyer of delight—
the Self, the living soul, always near,
lord of what was and what will be—
no longer hides in fear.[59]

The Purpose of Life

The Upanishads state that the purpose of life is to realize Brahman, the wholeness of life first discovered in the Self and eventually perceived as the common constituent of every particle of creation. In the Chāndogya Upanishad, when the young Shvetaketu was returning home from his studies, his father asks him, "When you know one lump of clay, you know everything made out of clay. Do you know that, by knowing which, everything becomes known?"[60] Shvetaketu then asks for instruction, and his father teaches him the unbounded nature of the Self and its identity with Brahman.

Dr. Radhakrishnan points out that "Brahman is not merely a featureless Absolute. It is all this world."[61] Therefore, to realize Brahman is not life denying, but affirming the identity of oneself with the world. Then one can say, "I am everything," or in the beautiful words of the Shvetāshvatara Upanishad:

You are woman. You are man.
You are the youth and the maiden too.
You are the old man hobbling along with a staff.
Once born, you are the face turned in every direction.

You are the dark blue butterfly,
you are the green parrot with red eyes.

You are the thundercloud, pregnant with lightning.
You are the seasons, you are the seas. You are without beginning,
present everywhere. You, from whom all worlds are born.[62]

Shankara's Commentary on the Upanishads

Shankara examined the various trends of thought found in the Upanishads and taught a philosophy that came to be known as nondualistic Vedānta. His understanding of the literature still shapes the central teaching of the Veda in India. Shankara based his teaching on a threefold textual foundation, called the *prasthāna traya*: the Upanishads, Brahma Sūtras and Bhagavad-Gītā. Shankara wrote commentaries on each of these, and therefore he is known as a teacher (*āchārya*) and is referred to as "Shankarāchārya."[63]

Shankara begins his commentary on the Upanishads by writing, "The sole purpose of all the Upanishads is to determine the nature of Ātman."[64] He describes Ātman as eternal, unchanging, undifferentiated, omnipresent and constant, because it cannot be created (*utpādya*), it cannot be transformed (*saṁskārya*), it cannot be grasped (*āpya*) like an object, and it cannot be damaged or destroyed (*vikārya*).[65]

Probably the most well-known teaching of Shankara is the principle of illusion, or *māyā*. Shankara defines māyā as "that which (*yā*) is not (*mā*)." According to Shankara, māyā is rooted in ignorance (*avidyā*), which is to say that māyā is due to ignorance of the state of unified awareness. According to Shankara, ignorance is caused by superimposition (*adhyāsa*), which he defines as an apparent presentation (*avabhāsa*) to consciousness by way of remembrance (*smṛiti-rūpa*) of something previously perceived (*pūrva-drishta*) somewhere else. In short, he defines māyā as the condition of perception dominated by memory. For example, someone may be filled with fear not because of a present threat, but because of a remembered threat. In other words, a person fails to see the distinction between the threat of an actual tiger and the memory of a tiger. Both are experienced as a real threat. Modern neurophysiologists might associate this with a hyperactive amygdala, which locks a person in the fight-or-flight response. For Shankara, this condition affects everyone to some degree, except those who have gained liberation (*moksha*). Shankara teaches that memory covers the perception of infinity, which is right in front of us. This covering is māyā, illusion.

Perhaps one might ask, "What if there is a clear danger, such as a fatal sickness?" Shankara's answer would be that the essential nature of the Self is unbounded consciousness, which can never be endangered because it is an immortal reality. The suffering that one perceives is due to the lack of perception of one's essential nature. For Shankara, all illusion is rooted in ignorance of the true reality, which is Brahman. The illusion of ignorance can be changed when an individual's reality is changed, like the darkness that is removed when the light is brought in.

Superimposition is the situation where the reality of Brahman is covered up by a false, inaccurate perception of reality. Shankara taught that superimposition is only an appearance (*vivarta*), like a string that appears to be a snake. In reality, there is only a string; in reality, there is only Brahman.

According to Vedānta, Brahman is without qualities, although it has three essential characteristics: existence, consciousness and bliss (*sat chit ānanda*). These qualities are not considered descriptions of Brahman, but the essential nature of Brahman. While Brahman is said to be indescribable, Shankara highlights many words from the Upanishads to describe it: one (*eka*), full (*pūrṇa*), all-encompassing (*paribhū*), all-pervading (*vibhū*), vast (*mahāntam*), omnipresent (*sarvagata*), supreme (*parama*), without end (*ananta*), without beginning (*anādi*), eternal (*nitya*), undivided (*abheda*), self-existent (*svayambhū*), self-luminous (*svaprakāsha*), imperishable (*akshara*), unchangeable (*avyaya*), indestructible (*anāshya*), inconceivable (*achintya*), unshakeable (*kūtastha*), immovable (*achala*) and constant (*dhruva*).

The Īsha Upanishad states that Brahman "is far, yet is within" (*tad dūre tad vantike*).[66] The Chāndogya Upanishad states that Brahman is "one reality without a second" (*ekam evādvitīyam*).[67] This last passage indicates why Shankara calls reality *advaita* or nondual.

Shankara states that the world by itself cannot be real (*sat*) because it is impermanent. However, since the world can be perceived, it cannot be unreal (*asat*) either. It cannot be completely nonexistent because we have an experience of it. Shankara states in his commentary on the Brahma Sūtras, "It can never be that what is actually perceived is non-existent."[68] Therefore, he declares that the world is neither real nor unreal (*satasat*).

Our experience of the world, according to Shankara, has been superimposed upon Brahman, which is the true reality. The false perception of the world as separate from Brahman is ignorance. As the Shvetāshvatara Upanishad beautifully expresses, ignorance is not the perception of diversity itself, but the perception of diversity separated from oneself:

In the vast wheel of Brahman in which all things live and rest,
the swan, the self, flutters about,
thinking himself and the mover to be separate.[69]

The consequence of perceiving diversity without unified awareness is becoming bound to the cycle of birth and rebirth (*saṁsāra*), as described in the Katha Upanishad: "He goes from death to death who sees even a hint of difference here."[70]

Shankara states that when Brahman is permanently experienced by the individual, there is liberation, the goal of human existence. The liberation that results from the realization of Brahman is often described in the Upanishads:

He who knows this Brahman, the supreme, the immortal,
set in the cave of the heart, my gentle friend,
cuts the knot of ignorance in this very life.[71]

"The purpose served by the scripture," Shankara states, "is that it enables one to attain the knowledge of the identity of Ātman with Brahman and thereby destroys grief and delusion, which are the result of ignorance."[72] He quotes the *mahāvākyas*, especially "Thou art that" (*tat tvam asi*),[73] to illustrate that Brahman is not an outer reality that one comes to know, but rather one realizes that one's Self is the reality. This is why the Muṇdaka Upanishad says, "The knower of Brahman is Brahman itself" (*brahmavid brahmaiva bhavati*).[74] Brahman is the knower and the known joined together, as described eloquently by Professor Eliot Deutsch: "Brahman is that state which *is* when all subject/object distinctions are obliterated. Brahman is ultimately a name for the experience of the timeless plenitude of being."[75] Brahman, the wholeness of unity and diversity, pierces the illusion of māyā.

Some of Shankara's followers changed his understanding of māyā to mean that the world is an illusion in and of itself. An extreme case of this was the doctrine put forth by a follower of Shankara, called *dṛishti-sṛishti-vāda*, which maintains that there is no world independent of one's perception of it. This is subjective idealism, where "I close my eyes and you disappear." Often the use of the word *māyā* as illusion refers to this concept, which is different from Shankara's original teaching and caused Shankara to be dismissed by people who were interested in practical living.

Maharishi Mahesh Yogi's Contribution to the Upanishads

Maharishi Mahesh Yogi came from the Shankarāchārya tradition of India. For thirteen years he was a disciple of the Shankarāchārya of Jyotirmath, Swami Brahmānanda Saraswatī.[76] For five decades after that, Maharishi traveled the world, teaching the wisdom of the Himālayas to people from all walks of life and establishing educational institutions on every continent. Maharishi remarked, "It is my joy to make the difficult simple." This was his contribution in many areas of the literature, including the Upanishads. Maharishi has taken the ancient wisdom of the Upanishads and integrated it into a complete science of consciousness, available in a systematic and empirically based body of knowledge. He once said, "The study of the Upanishads is the flow of our life."[77]

For Maharishi, the Upanishads are fundamentally about the knowledge and experience of transcending, which he made available by bringing to light the Transcendental Meditation technique.[78] Transcendental Meditation allows people to experience a state of pure consciousness, a state beyond thought in which the mind is awake, experiencing lively silence and nothing else. The Upanishads often mention this state of consciousness, which they call *turīya chetanā*, or the fourth, because it follows the three better known states of consciousness: waking, dreaming and sleeping. Turīya is also known as *samādhi* in the Upanishads and especially in the literature of yoga. The Māṇḍūkya Upanishad speaks of this state of pure consciousness as "peaceful, benign, undivided—that is known as the fourth. That is the Self. That is to be realized."[79] This state is first realized during meditation, illustrating that the Upanishads offer not just a philosophy, but a description of direct experience. Because the fourth state of consciousness is measurable and repeatable, it is open to the systematic procedures of verification found in science.

Maharishi emphasizes that turīya is the gateway to higher states of consciousness. With regular practice of meditation, the fourth state of consciousness begins to be experienced simultaneously with the waking, dreaming and sleeping states of consciousness. Eventually, consciousness becomes a living reality—one perceives every object of attention as pure consciousness. Maharishi describes this as *Unity Consciousness* (*brāhmī chetanā*), where there is an experiential unity between the perceiver and the object of perception, based on the initial experience of the Self in the fourth state of consciousness.

For Maharishi, Unity Consciousness means living a fully integrated life in activity. Like Shankara, Maharishi does not regard creation as an illusion, which was taught by some of Shankara's followers. Maharishi writes about the fate of Shankara's teaching at the hands of his followers: "The teaching became one-sided and, deprived of its wholeness, eventually lost its universal appeal. It came to be regarded as *māyāvāda,* a philosophy of illusion, holding the world to be only illusory and emphasizing the detached way of life."[80]

Maharishi explains that for one who is experiencing unity, the world is Brahman, not an illusion: "The world was a mirage only in so far as it was experienced as different from one's Self."[81] For those who are in the ordinary waking state of consciousness, the lack of holistic awareness produces experience dominated by diversity, but as Maharishi points out, "Once that lack is removed, the world of differences is the world of wholeness."[82] Diversity may appear to be an obstacle at one stage of life, but from the reality of Unity Consciousness, the variety of the world is an ever-increasing joy.

Maharishi emphasizes that the material creation is nothing other than consciousness itself. It is only in the state of ignorance that diversity appears to be distinct from that ultimate reality of Brahman. In the state of enlightenment, the world is experienced and understood to be wholeness, Brahman. The illusion is not the existence of creation, but rather the illusion is the inaccurate perception that creation is separate from wholeness.

Brahman is unity. It is one reality composed of unmanifest and manifest existence. This fundamental principle of the Upanishads is found in the phrase, "That is full; this is full" (*pūrṇam adaḥ pūrṇam idam*).[83] Maharishi explains that "this and that," the unmoving and the moving, are two parts of existence:

> The eternal texts of the Vedas, crowned with the philosophy of the Upanishads, reveal the relative and the Absolute as two aspects of the one reality, Brahman, absolute Being, which, although unmanifest in Its essential nature, manifests as relative creation."[84]

According to Vedānta, the inherent nature of life is eternal bliss consciousness (*sat chit ānanda*), which can be seen in a passage that Maharishi emphasized from the Taittirīya Upanishad: "Out of bliss these beings are born, in bliss they are sustained, and to bliss they go and merge again."[85] The joy of life, the bedrock of the Upanishads, is also the essential message of Maharishi's teaching, as shown in one of his first books, *The Science of Being and Art of Living*, which says, "Expansion of happiness is the purpose of creation."[86] He clearly states that life is essentially bliss in nature:

> I hold that life is bliss. In essence life is not a struggle. Man is not born to suffer, but to feel joyful; he is born of bliss, consciousness, wisdom and creativity. Once the flower of life has bloomed in a man, then consciousness, wisdom and creativity are ever-present in him. When the inner, or spiritual, and the outer, or material,

glories of life are consciously brought into harmony, then life is integrated and becomes truly worth living.[87]

Perhaps Maharishi's greatest contribution to the Upanishads is to point out that they describe a living reality that can be experienced. They are an authentic record of the ultimate meaning of existence, which is first experienced in turīya and later established in the state of Unity Consciousness. According to Maharishi, the purpose of the Upanishads is to offer a vision of the most profound truths of life and to inspire people to live these truths in their day-to-day life. Maharishi explains that *upanishad*, "sit down near," is the description of Unity Consciousness, because in that state everything sits down near the speaker, who perceives the infinite correlation between all things. In Unity Consciousness, everything is the Self, which the Upanishads describe as the living experience of seeing "all beings in the Self and the Self in all beings."[88]

The Upanishads make clear that the highest realization is linked to the repeated experience of the fourth state of consciousness (turīya). For example, in the Shvetāshvatara Upanishad, the sage Shvetāshvatara describes how he realized unity "through the power of meditation and through the grace of God."[89] First the Self is realized in isolation and then as the ultimate reality in all things. The Upanishads describe the person aspiring for unity as "using the nature of his own Self (*Ātmā*) like a lamp to illumine the true nature of Brahman."[90] The present translation of the Upanishads was undertaken with this reality in mind and heart.

—Thomas Egenes

Īsha Upanishad[1]

That is full; this is full.[2]
From fullness, fullness comes out.
Taking fullness from fullness,
what remains is fullness.[3]
Oṁ shāntiḥ shāntiḥ shāntiḥ

1.
Everything here, whatever moves
in the moving world, is pervaded by the Lord.
Enjoy it by way of relinquishing it;
cease to take for yourself what to others are riches.[4]

2.
Always performing actions here,
one may aspire to live a hundred years.
Thus for you there is no other way than this,
whereby action will not cling to you.

3.
Sunless are those worlds called,
covered in blinding darkness;
there, after departing, go those men
who are slayers of the Self.[5]

4.
It is one, unmoving, swifter than the mind.
The senses cannot reach it. It darts ahead.
Standing still, it outruns those who run.
Within it the breath of life supports all that stirs.

5.
It moves and it moves not.
It is far away and it is close by.[6]
It is within all this.
It is outside all this.

6.
He who sees
all beings in the Self
and the Self in all beings
no longer hides in fear.[7]

7.
For the man of wisdom,
in whom all beings have become his own Self,
how can delusion, how can sorrow
befall that seer of oneness?

8.
He is all-pervading, shining, bodiless, unscarred, without sinews, pure, untouched by sin. He is the seer, wise, encompassing all, self-existent. Through endless time he has ordained objects in due succession.

9.
Into blinding darkness enter
those who worship ignorance.
Into as if still greater darkness
enter those who delight in knowledge.[8]

10.
"It is other than knowledge," they say.
"It is other than ignorance," they say.
Thus we have heard from the wise
who have explained it to us.

11.
Knowledge and ignorance—
he who knows both together,[9]
crosses beyond mortality through ignorance
and attains immortality through knowledge.

12.
Into blinding darkness
enter those who worship the unmanifest.
Into as if still greater darkness
enter those who delight in the manifest.

13.
"It is other than existence," they say.
"It is other than nonexistence," they say.
Thus have we heard from the wise
who have explained it to us.

14.
Manifest and unmanifest—
he who knows both together,
crosses beyond death through the unmanifest
and attains immortality through the manifest.

15.
The face of truth
is hidden by a disc of gold.[10]
Unveil it, O Pūshan, so that I,
steadfast in truth, may see.

16.
O Pūshan, the sole seer, O controller, O Sūrya, offspring
of Prajāpati, disperse your rays and gather in your light,
so that I may behold your most graceful form.
He who is that person afar, I am he.[11]

17.
Let this life-breath join with the immortal breath.
Then let this body end in ashes. *Om.* Remember, O my
understanding, remember what has been done. Remember,
O my understanding, what has been done, remember.

18.
Agni, lead us by the good path to prosperity,
O radiant one, who knows all our ways.
Remove from us our crooked sins.
May we offer you abundant words of praise.[12]

That is full; this is full.
From fullness, fullness comes out.
Taking fullness from fullness,
what remains is fullness.
Oṁ shāntiḥ shāntiḥ shāntiḥ

Kena Upanishad[1]

May my limbs, speech, breath,
eyes, ears abound in vigor,
also my strength and all my senses.

All is Brahman, revealed in the Upanishads.
May I never reject Brahman.
May Brahman never reject me.
May there be no rejection.
May there be no rejection of me.
May those truths in the Upanishads
abide in me, who delight in the Self.
Oṁ shāntiḥ shāntiḥ shāntiḥ

First Khaṇḍa

1.

[Pupil:] Willed by whom, propelled by whom, does the mind take wing? Willed by whom does the breath march on,

preceding all? Willed by whom do people utter speech?
What radiant being[2] engages eye and ear?

2.
[Teacher:] He is the ear of the ear, the mind of the mind,
the speech of speech, the breath of the breath,
the eye of the eye. Liberated, the wise,
giving up this world, become immortal.

3.
There the eye goes not,
speech goes not, nor the mind.
We know not, we comprehend not,
how anyone could teach this.

It is other than the known;
it is also beyond the unknown.
Thus we have heard from the ancients,
who have revealed it to us.[3]

4.
That which is not uttered by speech,
but by which speech is uttered—
that alone know to be Brahman,
not what people venerate here.

5.
That which is not thought by the mind,
but by which, they say, thought is thought—

that alone know to be Brahman,
not what people venerate here.

6.
That which is not seen with the eye,
but by which the eye sees—
that alone know to be Brahman,
not what people venerate here.

7.
That which is not heard by the ear,
but by which hearing is heard—
that alone know to be Brahman,
not what people venerate here.

8.
That which is not breathed by breath,
but by which breath is breathed—
that alone know to be Brahman,
not what people venerate here.

Second Khaṇḍa

1.
[Teacher:] If you think, "I know it well," then you surely know only very little of the nature of Brahman—whether it relates to you or to the gods. So it is still to be pondered on by you.

[Pupil:] I think it is known.

2.
I do not think, "I know it well,"
nor do I know, "I know it not."
He among us who realizes, "Not that I do not know—
I know it and I know it not," he knows it.[4]

3.
[Teacher:] To whom it is not known, to him it is known.
To whom it is known, he knows it not.
It is not understood by those who understand.
It is understood by those who do not understand.

4.
When known through an awakening,
it is rightly known; thus one gains immortality.
Through the Self one gains strength,[5]
through knowledge, immortality.

5.
If one has realized it in this life, then there is truth;
if one has not realized it here, great is the loss.
Wise men, who have perceived it in being after being
and have turned away from this world,[6] become immortal.

THIRD KHAṆḌA

1.
Brahman once won a victory for the gods, and the gods reveled in that victory which belonged to Brahman. They thought to themselves, "Ours alone is this victory, ours alone, this glory."

2.
Now Brahman knew this of them and appeared before them. They did not recognize him and said, "Who is this wondrous being (*yaksha*)?"

3.
They said to Agni, "O Jātavedas, find out who is this wondrous being."

"So be it," he said.

4.
He hurried toward it, and it said to him, "Who are you?"

"I assuredly am Agni.[7] I am Jātavedas," he replied.

5.
"What power is there in one such as you?" the being asked.

"I can burn everything here with ease, whatever there is on earth," Agni replied.

6.
Then the being placed a straw before him, saying, "Burn this."

Agni rushed toward it with all speed. He could not burn it. He returned from there saying, "I could not discover who is this wondrous being."

7.
Then the gods said to Vāyu, "O Vāyu, find out who is this wondrous being."

"So be it," he said.

8.

He hurried toward it, and it said to him, "Who are you?"

"I assuredly am Vāyu.[8] I am Mātarishvan," he replied.

9.

"What power is there in one such as you?" the being asked.

"I can blow away everything here with ease, whatever there is on earth," Vāyu replied.

10.

Then the wondrous being placed a straw before him, saying, "Blow this away."

Vāyu rushed toward it with all speed. He could not blow it away. He returned from there saying, "I could not discover who is this wondrous being."

11.

Then the gods said to Indra, "O Maghavan, find out who is this wondrous being."

"So be it," he said. He hurried toward it. It vanished before him.

12.

In that very space Indra came upon a most beautiful woman, Umā, daughter of the Himālaya.

He said to her, "Who is that wondrous being?"

Fourth Khaṇḍa

1\.
"It is Brahman," she replied. "It is surely in the victory of Brahman that you attained your glory." Only from that moment did Indra recognize that this was Brahman.

2\.
Therefore these gods—Agni, Vāyu and Indra—greatly surpass, as it were, the other gods, for they came closest to it; they first recognized this was Brahman.

3\.
That indeed is why Indra greatly surpasses, as it were, the other gods, for he came closest to it; he first recognized this was Brahman.

4\.
Of it there is this teaching: It is like a flash of lightning; it is like the twinkling of an eye. This is concerning the gods.

5\.
Now concerning the self: Brahman is that toward which the mind moves, as it were, that by which it is ever aware and that which forms its purpose.

6\.
It is known as that which is greatly beloved, and as the beloved it should be venerated. All beings surely long for him who knows it as this.

7.
[Pupil:] "Revered Sir, tell me the secret knowledge."

[Teacher:] "The secret knowledge has been told to you. We have taught you the secret knowledge of Brahman."

8.
Meditation, self-command and Vedic performance are its foundation; the Vedas are all its limbs; truth is its dwelling.

9.
He who truly knows this as such, casting off sin, is established in the world of heaven,[9] boundless and invincible. Indeed, he is established.

May my limbs, speech, breath,
eyes, ears, abound in vigor,
also my strength and all my senses.

All is Brahman, revealed in the Upanishads.
May I never reject Brahman.
May Brahman never reject me.
May there be no rejection.
May there be no rejection of me.
May those truths that are in the Upanishads
abide in me, who delight in the Self.
Oṁ shāntiḥ shāntiḥ shāntiḥ

Katha Upanishad[1]

Let us be together.
Let us eat together.
Let us be vital together.
Let us be radiating truth,
radiating the light of life.
Never shall we denounce anyone,
never entertain negativity.[2]
Oṁ shāntiḥ shāntiḥ shāntiḥ

First Adhyāya

First Vallī

1.
At one time, Vājashravasa, desirous of reward, gave away all his possessions. He had a son, Nachiketas by name.

2.
As the gifts were being taken away, faith entered Nachiketas. Though still a boy, he said to himself:

3.
"They have drunk their water, eaten their grass,
given their milk, they can no longer calve—
one who gives such cows as gifts
goes to worlds that are joyless indeed."

4.
Then he said to his father, "Father, to whom will you give me?" He said it a second, a third time. Then his father said to him, "To Death will I give you."

5.
[Nachiketas:] Of many, I rank as first;
of many, I rank as middling.[3]
What purpose of Yama[4]
will my father accomplish through me today?

6.
Consider how it was with men of old;
observe how it is with others today.
Like grain a mortal dies;
like grain he is born again.[5]

7.
[Yama's counselors:] A Brāhmaṇa[6] guest
enters homes like fire,

and they make peace with him in this way:
"Bring water, O son of Vivasvat."[7]

8.
From the man of little wisdom in whose home he stays,
unfed, a Brāhmaṇa snatches away hope and expectation,
friendship[8] and true delight,[9] the fruit of rites
and good actions, also sons and cattle—all this.

9.
[Yama:] O Brāhmaṇa, since you, a guest worthy of honor,
have stayed in my home for three nights unfed,
I pay homage to you, O Brāhmaṇa. May good fortune be mine.
Choose then three boons.

10.
[Nachiketas:] O Death, may Gautama [my father]
feel peaceful toward me, well-disposed and free from anger.
May he acknowledge and welcome me, when released by you.
I choose this as the first of the three boons.

11.
[Yama:] Your father, Auddālaki Āruṇi,[10] released [from anger]
by me, will acknowledge you as of old.
Seeing you liberated from the mouth of death,
he will rest well through the nights, his anger gone.

12.
[Nachiketas:] In the world of heaven there is no fear at all;
you are not present,[11] nor does one fear old age.
Having passed beyond both hunger and thirst,
and left sorrow behind, one rejoices in the heavenly world.

13.
You understand that (sacrificial) fire which leads to heaven.
O Death, explain it to me, for I have faith.
Those in the heavenly world enjoy immortality.
This I choose for my second boon.

14.
[Yama:] Knowing well the fire that leads to heaven,
I will explain it to you. Pay heed to me, Nachiketas.
Know it as the way to win the boundless world, as the stay
of the universe, as that which dwells in the cave of the heart.

15.
He described to him that fire, the source of the world,
what bricks, how many and how arranged.
And Nachiketas repeated it just as it was told.
Then, satisfied with him, Death spoke again.

16.
The great soul (Yama), well pleased, said to him,
"Here, this day, I grant you a further boon:
By your name alone shall this fire be known.
Accept also this necklace of many facets.

17.
"One who has kindled the Nāchiketas[12] fire three times,
who has gained union with the three,[13]
who has performed the threefold duties,[14]
crosses over birth and death. Having understood the
all-knowing one, born of Brahmā,[15] shining,
adorable, and realizing him,[16] he gains unbroken peace.

18.
"He who kindles the Nāchiketas fire three times, having known these three, with this knowledge completes the Nāchiketas rite. He throws off the fetters of death before [leaving the body] and, crossing beyond sorrow, rejoices in the world of heaven.

19.
"This is your fire, Nachiketas, leading to heaven,
which you have chosen as your second boon.
Men will speak of this fire as yours alone.
Choose, Nachiketas, the third boon."

20.
[Nachiketas:] When a man departs, there is this uncertainty.
Some say, "He is," others, "He is not."
This knowledge I wish to receive, with you as my teacher.
This is the third of my boons.

21.
[Yama:] Since ancient times, even the gods have been
uncertain about this, for this truth is subtle,
not easy to understand. Nachiketas, choose another boon.
Do not press me. Release me from this.

22.
[Nachiketas:] Since even the gods were uncertain about this,
and you, O Death, say it is not easy to know,
and since there is no other teacher of this who is your equal,
no other boon can compare to this.

23.
[Yama:] Choose sons and grandsons who will live
a hundred years. Choose many cows, choose elephants,
gold and horses. Choose a vast expanse of land,
and yourself live as many autumns as you desire.

24.
If you think another boon equal, choose it.
Choose wealth and long life.
Prosper on this vast earth, Nachiketas.
I shall make you the enjoyer of all your desires.

25.
Whatever desires are hard to obtain in the world of mortals,
choose all these pleasures at your will. Here are fair maidens
with lutes and chariots, their like beyond the reach of

mortals. These I give you. Let them attend on you.
But about death, Nachiketas, do not ask.

26.
[Nachiketas:] These are fleeting, O Lord of Death,
and consume the fire of all a mortal's senses.
All life is but brief. Yours be the carriages,
yours the dance and song!

27.
Man will never be satisfied by wealth.
Shall we have wealth once we have seen you?
We shall only live as long as you ordain.
So that alone is the boon[17] to be chosen by me.

28.
Once he has met the immortals who do not age
and knows [their world], how could an aging mortal
on this lowly earth, pondering the delights of beauty
and love, rejoice in a life too long?

29.
That about which people are perplexed—
what happens at the great passing—tell us that, O Death.
That boon which pierces the secret,
none other than this does Nachiketas choose.

Second Vallī

1.
[Yama:] The good is one thing, the pleasurable surely another.
These two, with different goals, both bind a man.
Of these, good attends him who embraces the good.
Whoso chooses the pleasurable misses the true goal.

2.
The good and the pleasurable both approach a man.
Looking at them from every side, the wise man discriminates.
He chooses the good over the pleasurable.
The fool, clinging onto possessions, chooses the pleasurable.

3.
You have thought about objects of desire
that please or seem to please and have let them go, Nachiketas.
You have not taken up this way of wealth
on which many mortals perish.

4.
Far apart and going their different ways are these two,
ignorance and what is called knowledge.
I think Nachiketas is eager for knowledge—
the many objects of desire have not bewildered you.

5.
Living in the midst of ignorance,
wise in their own eyes, thinking themselves scholars,
fools go round and round, running here and there,
like the blind led by the blind.[18]

6.
Unaware of his own mortality, the childish one
stumbles about, enchanted by the folly of riches.
Thinking there is only this world and no other,
he falls again and again under my control.

7.
He[19] who by many cannot even be heard of,
whom many, even hearing, do not know—
wonderful is the one who teaches him, skilled the one
who grasps him, wonderful the knower skillfully taught.

8.
Taught by an inferior man, this Self cannot be easily known,
even though often reflected upon. Unless taught by one
who knows him as none other than his own Self,
there is no way to him, for he is subtler than subtle,
beyond the range of reasoning.

9.
Not by logic can this realization be won. Only when taught
by another, [an enlightened teacher],[20] is it easily known,
dearest friend. You have attained it, Nachiketas, for you are
steadfast in truth. May we always find a questioner like you.

10.
What is called treasure,[21] I know to be transient,
for the changeless cannot be won by the changing.
Still, the Nāchiketas fire has been piled up by me:
through perishable things I have won what is imperishable.[22]

11.
Gratification of desire, the foundation of the world,
power beyond measure, the other shore beyond fear,
the height of praise, the far extending, the basis—
having observed these, wise Nachiketas,
you have firmly rejected them.

12.
The wise man, who through the practice of union with the
Self, has realized that ancient effulgent being, who is hidden,
not obvious to perception, set in the secret place of the heart,
lodged in the depths—that man leaves joy and sorrow behind.

13.
When a mortal has heard this and understood it well,
when he has separated out his essential nature
and attained this finest point,
then he rejoices, for he has won what is worthy of joy.
I think the home [of Brahman] is wide open to Nachiketas.

14.
[Nachiketas:] That which you see as beyond right and wrong,
beyond what has and has not been done,
beyond what was and what will be—
tell me that.

15.
[Yama:] The goal which all the Vedas proclaim,
which all austerities speak of,

desiring which, people practice self-restraint,
that goal I will tell you in brief. It is *Om*.

16.
This imperishable indeed is Brahman.
This imperishable indeed is the supreme.
For one who truly knows this imperishable,
whatever he desires is his.

17.
This is the best support.
This is the highest support.
Knowing this support,
one is exalted in the world of Brahman.

18.
The conscious Self is never born, nor does he ever die.
He came out of nothing and nothing has come out of him.
Unborn, eternal, everlasting, ancient,
he is not slain when the body is slain.[23]

19.
If the slayer thinks he slays,
and if the slain thinks he is being slain,
both fail to perceive the truth.
He [the Self] neither slays nor is slain.[24]

20.
Smaller than the smallest, greater than the greatest,[25]
the Self is lodged in the heart of every being. The man
free of contriving, through calmness of mind and senses,
sees the majesty of the Self and leaves sorrow behind.

21.
Sitting, he travels far.
Reclining, he goes everywhere.[26]
Who else but I can know
that radiant being who rejoices and rejoices not?

22.
Bodiless amidst bodies,
stable amidst the unstable—
having known the vast, all-pervading Self,
the wise man does not grieve.

23.
This Self cannot be attained by instruction,
nor by the intellect, nor yet by much learning.
He is attained only by one whom he chooses.[27]
To him, this Self uncovers his own nature.[28]

24.
He who has not discarded wrong action,
who is not tranquil, who is not collected,
whose mind is not at peace,
cannot attain this Self through knowledge.

25.
He for whom both priest (*brāhmaṇa*)
and noble (*kshatriya*) are food,
and death is but a curry—
who really knows where he is?

Third Vallī

1.
There are two[29] who drink truth in the world of good deeds.[30]
Both are lodged in the cave of the heart,
the foremost dwelling of the supreme.
Knowers of Brahman speak of them as shadow and light,
so also do those [householders] who keep the five fires
and those who thrice kindle the Nāchiketas fire.

2.
We are able to perform the Nāchiketas fire,
which is the bridge for those who sacrifice, and we are
able to know the supreme imperishable Brahman, sought
by those who long to cross to the further shore, beyond fear.

3.
Know the Self as the master of the chariot
and the body as the chariot.
Know the intellect as the charioteer
and the mind as the reins.

4.
The senses, they say, are the horses;
sense objects, the ground they cover.
[The Self], when joined with body, mind and senses,
the wise call the enjoyer.

5.
When a man lacks right judgment,
and his mind is not collected,
then his senses run out of control,
like the wild horses of a charioteer.

6.
But when he has right judgment
and a mind that is ever collected,
then his senses come under control,
like the good horses of a charioteer.

7.
When a man lacks right judgment,
and is unmindful, ever impure,
then he fails to reach the goal
and treads the round of birth and death.

8.
But when he has right judgment
and is mindful, ever pure,
then he reaches that place
from where he is not born again.

9.
One who has right judgment as his charioteer,
who reins in his mind,
reaches the end of the journey,
that highest place of Vishṇu.[31]

10.
Beyond the senses are their objects;
beyond the objects is the mind;
but beyond the mind is the intellect;
beyond the intellect is the great self.[32]

11.
Beyond the great is the unmanifest;[33]
beyond the unmanifest is Purusha;[34]
beyond Purusha there is nothing.
That is the end; that is the highest goal.

12.
Hidden in all beings,
the Self is not visible to the eye,
but it is seen by seers of subtle vision
through their pointed, subtle intellect.

13.
The wise one should retire speech into mind,
the mind he should retire into the intelligent self.[35]
The intelligent self he should withdraw into the great self,
the great self he should retire into the Self of peace.[36]

14.
Arise! Awake! Seek out the best teachers,[37]
learn well, for that path is narrow,
sharp as the edge of a razor,
unfathomable, so the sages declare.[38]

15.
That which is without sound, without touch, without form,
without taste, without smell, unchanging, eternal, which is
without beginning or end, beyond the great,[39] constant—
by perceiving that, one is released from the mouth of death.

16.
The wise man, who has heard and told
the immortal story of Nachiketas,
narrated by Death,
is glorified in the world of Brahmā.

17.
Whoever devoutly proclaims this supreme secret
before a gathering of Brāhmaṇas
or during the *shrāddha* offering[40]
receives an infinite reward. Yes, he receives an infinite reward.

Second Adhyāya

First Vallī

1.
The Self-existent pierced the openings [of the senses] outward;
therefore one looks outside, not within oneself.
A certain wise man, seeking eternal life,
turned his eyes inward and saw the Self directly.

2.
The childish go after outward pleasures
and fall into the net of death spread wide.
But the wise, who have known the immortal,
look not for the changeless in this ever-changing world.

3.
Through that [Self] alone
one experiences form, taste, smell,
sound, touch and sexual union.
What else remains here?
  This indeed is that.

4.
Having known the great, all-pervading Self,
by which one experiences
in both the sleep and waking states,
the wise man does not grieve.

5.
He who knows this enjoyer of delight—
the Self, the living soul, always near,
lord of what was and what will be—
no longer hides in fear.[41]
This indeed is that.

6.
He who was born of radiance in the beginning,
who was born before the waters,
who entered the cave of the heart and dwells there,
and perceived [the world] through living beings—
This indeed is that.[42]

7.
She who arises with the breath of life,
Aditi, embodiment of divinity,
who entered the cave of the heart and dwells there,
who was born through living beings—
This indeed is that.

8.
Agni, the all-knowing, hidden in the two fire-sticks
like an embryo safely guarded by pregnant women,
should be adored day-by-day by awakened men
and by those who offer oblations.
This indeed is that.

9.
That from which the sun rises,
and where it goes to set—
in that all the gods are placed.[43]
No one ever passes beyond it.
    This indeed is that.

10.
Whatever is here, that is there.
What is there, that is also here.
He meets with death after death
who sees even a hint of difference here.[44]

11.
Only by the mind can this be realized—
there is no diversity here at all.
He goes from death to death
who sees even a hint of difference here.

12.
Purusha, the size of a thumb,
dwells in the center of the body.
On knowing him, the lord of what was
and what will be, one no longer hides in fear.
    This indeed is that.

13.
Purusha, the size of a thumb,
like a flame without smoke,

lord of what was and what will be—
he is the same today as tomorrow.
  This indeed is that.

14.
As rain fallen on a rugged peak
rushes down the mountainsides in scattered streams,
so he who sees objects as separate,
rushes after them in all directions.

15.
As pure water poured
into pure water is one and the same,
so it is with the Self of the seer
who knows, O Gautama.

SECOND VALLĪ

1.
There is a city of eleven gates[45] that belongs
to the unborn, unwavering consciousness.
One who is absorbed in him sorrows not,
and set free, he is free.[46]
  This indeed is that.

2.
As the sun he lives in the heavens,
  as air he lives in the atmosphere,
  as fire he lives on earth,
  as a guest he lives in the home.

He lives in man, he lives in the gods,
he lives in truth, he lives in space.
Born in water, born in earth born in the rite,
born in the mountains, he is the true,
he is the great.

3.
He sends the out-breath (*prāṇa*) upward.
He drives the in-breath (*apāna*) inward.
All the senses (*deva*) serve him,
the dwarf,[47] seated in the center.

4.
When the dweller in the body,
the body's owner, becomes detached,
released from the body,
what more remains here?
This indeed is that.

5.
Not by the out-breath nor by the in-breath
does any mortal live.
They live by virtue of another,
on which these breaths depend.

6.
Pay heed, I shall declare to you, O Gautama,
this secret, the eternal Brahman,
and what becomes of the soul
once death is reached.

7.
Some souls enter a womb
to obtain a body,
others pass into something motionless[48]—
each according to his deeds, according to his knowledge.

8.
The indweller (Purusha) who lies awake in those who sleep,
shaping desire after desire—that alone is the pure.
That is Brahman. That indeed is called the immortal.
In it all worlds rest; beyond it no one ever passes.
This indeed is that.

9.
Just as a single fire, entering the world,
assumes the likeness of form after form,
so the one Self within all beings
assumes the likeness of form after form, yet is beyond form.

10.
Just as the one air, entering the world,
assumes the likeness of form after form,
so the one Self within all beings
assumes the likeness of form after form, yet is beyond form.

11.
Just as the sun, which illuminates the whole world,
is not touched by outside blemishes seen by the eyes,
so the Self within all beings is not touched
by the sorrows of the world, for it lies beyond them.

12.
He who is the one ruler, the Self within all beings,
who makes his one form into many,
him the wise recognize as present within themselves.
They, and no others, have lasting happiness.

13.
He who is the changeless in the ever-changing,
the consciousness in conscious beings, who dispenses desired
objects to the many, him the wise recognize as present
within themselves. They, and no others, have lasting peace.

14.
"This is that"—thus they understand
the highest happiness which is beyond expression.
How then may I know that?
Does it shine of itself or does it shine by another?

15.
There the sun shines not, nor the moon nor stars,
nor do these lightnings shine, much less this fire.
Only when he shines does everything shine.
This whole world shines by his light.[49]

THIRD VALLĪ

1.
Its roots above, its branches spread below—
this is the eternal *ashvattha* tree.[50] That[51] indeed is the pure.
That is Brahman. That indeed is called the immortal.
In it all worlds rest; beyond it no one ever passes.[52]
    This indeed is that.

2.
This whole world, whatever there is,
having emerged, pulsates in *prāṇa*,[53]
who is like a great terror, an upraised thunderbolt.
They who know this become immortal.

3.
From fear of him, fire burns.
From fear, the sun blazes.
From fear, they take flight:
Indra and wind and death, the fifth.[54]

4.
If one can realize it in this life,
before the body breaks up, [he is freed];
[if not], he will assume another body
in one of the created worlds.

5.
In oneself it is seen as in a looking glass,[55]
in the world of the fathers as in a dream,
in the world of the *gandharvas* as though in water,
in the world of Brahmā as though in light and shade.[56]

6.
Knowing that the senses are distinct [from the Self],
each sense with its separate origin,
and that coming and going is their nature,[57]
the wise man does not grieve.

7.
Beyond the senses is the mind.
Higher than the mind is the intellect.
Above the intellect is the great self.
Higher than the great [self] is the unmanifest.

8.
And beyond the unmanifest is Purusha,
all-pervading and without any distinctive feature.
Knowing him, a person is set free
and reaches immortality.[58]

9.
His form is not within the range of vision.
No one sees him with the eyes.
With the heart, with the understanding, with the mind
is he seen.[59] They who know this become immortal.[60]

10.
When the five channels of knowledge
are at rest, together with the mind,
and the intellect does not stir,
they call that the highest state.

11.
The unwavering steadiness of the senses
they understand as yoga.
Then one becomes vigilant,
for yoga can be gained and lost.

12.
Not by speech, nor by mind,
nor by sight can that be reached.
How can it be known,
except from those who say, "It is."

13.
That should indeed be realized as "It is,"
and [then] as the true nature of both.[61]
Only for him who has realized "It is,"
does its true nature become clear.

14.
When all the desires
that cling to the heart fall away,
then a mortal becomes immortal
and realizes Brahman in this very life.[62]

15.
When all the knots of the heart
are severed here on earth,
then a mortal becomes immortal.
That is the complete teaching.

16.
A hundred and one are the channels of the heart.
Of these, one extends to the crown of the head.
Rising upward by that, one reaches immortality;
the rest, at the time of departing, lead in other directions.[63]

17.
The size of a thumb, Purusha, the inner Self, is ever seated
deep in the hearts of men. Him one should draw out
from one's body with steadiness, like the central stalk
from a blade of *munja* grass.
Him one should know as the pure, the immortal.
Yes, one should know him as the pure, the immortal.

18.
Then Nachiketas, having received this knowledge taught
by the Lord of Death, and also the entire way of yoga, having
been freed from impurity, freed from death, attained
Brahman.
And so will any other who knows this teaching of the Self.

Let us be together.
Let us eat together.
Let us be vital together.

Let us be radiating truth,
radiating the light of life.
Never shall we denounce anyone,
never entertain negativity.
Oṁ shāntiḥ shāntiḥ shāntiḥ

Prashna Upanishad[1]

All good I should hear from the ears, O radiant beings.
All good I should see through the eyes, O revered ones.
May we, full of praise, with bodies firm of limb,
enjoy the span of life given us by God.

May Indra, swelling in glory, grant us well-being.
May Pūshan, who knows all, grant us well-being.
May Tārkshya, who saves from harm, grant us well-being.
May Bṛihaspati confer upon us well-being.
Oṁ shāntiḥ shāntiḥ shāntiḥ

First Prashna

1.
Sukeshā, son of Bharadvāja; Satyakāma, son of Shibi; Gārgya, grandson of Sūrya; Kausalya, son of Ashvala; Bhārgava, from Vidarbha; and Kabandhī, descendant of Katya—these were men

devoted to Brahman, intent on Brahman, seeking the supreme Brahman. They approached the revered Pippalāda, firewood in hand,[2] thinking, "He will surely teach us all that."

2.
That seer said to them, "Live with me for the length of a year with austerity, celibacy and faith. Then ask questions as you wish. If we know, we will certainly tell you everything."

3.
Then Kabandhī, descendant of Katya, approached him and asked, "Revered Sir, from where do these creatures arise?"

4.
He answered him, "The lord of creation (Prajāpati) by nature longs for creatures, so he performed austerity. Having performed austerity, he created a pair—matter (*rayi*) and life (*prāṇa*)—thinking, 'These two will make creatures of many kinds for me.'

5.
"The sun, surely, is life; matter is the moon. Everything here, formed or unformed, is nothing but matter. So form is indeed matter.

6.
"Now the sun, as he rises, enters the eastern quarter. He thereby holds the creatures of the east within his rays. When he shines upon the southern, western and northern, the lower, upper and

intermediate regions—shines upon everything—then he holds creatures everywhere within his rays.

7.
"This is he who rises up as life, as fire, becoming all creatures, assuming all forms. It has been said in the Vedic hymn:

8.
"Assuming all forms, golden-hued, all-knowing,
the final refuge, the one light, the giver of heat—
so rises the sun, the thousand-rayed,
existing in a hundred ways, the breath of living beings.[3]

9.
"The year is indeed the lord of creation. His paths are two, the southern and the northern. Now those, indeed, thinking that devout sacrifices and pious deeds are their good works, win only the world of the moon. Surely they return again. Therefore those sages, who long for offspring, pass along the southern course. This is the realm of matter, which leads to the ancestors.

10.
"But those who seek the Self through austerity, celibacy, faith and knowledge, they, following the northern path, win the sun. That indeed is the sanctuary of all that lives. That is the immortal, free from fear. That is the final refuge. From that they do not come back. That is the end. Regarding it there is this verse:

11.
"Some speak of a father with five feet and twelve forms,
seated in the upper half of the sky, rich in moisture.
But others here call him the clear-sighted one,
placed on a chariot of seven wheels with six spokes.[4]

12.
"The month is surely the lord of creation. In this, the dark half is matter and the bright half, life. Therefore sages perform the sacrifice in the bright half, others in the dark half.

13.
"The cycle of day and night is the lord of creation (Prajāpati). In this, day is life and night, matter. They who join in physical union by day waste away life, but those who join in physical union by night are as good as chaste.

14.
"Food is the lord of creation. From that comes human seed; from that are born these living beings.

15.
"Therefore those who practice this rule[5] of the lord of creation produce a pair. That world of Brahman belongs to those who practice austerity and celibacy, in whom truth is established.

16.
"That stainless world of Brahman belongs to those
in whom there is no crookedness, falsehood or cunning."

Second Prashna

1.
Then Bhārgava from Vidarbha asked him, "Revered Sir, how many *devas* sustain a living being? Which of them illuminates this [body]? And who among them is the best?"

2.
He answered him, "Space surely is such a power (*deva*)—also air, fire, water, earth, speech, mind, sight and hearing. Having illuminated it, they declare, 'It is we who, holding this body,[6] sustain it.'

3.
"Life-breath (*prāṇa*), the leader, said to them, 'Do not fall into delusion. Dividing myself fivefold, it is I alone who holds this body and sustains it.' They did not believe him.

4.
"Through pride, he seemed to rise upward. As he rose, all the others rose too. As he settled down, all the others settled down too. Just as all the bees rise when the royal bee rises and settle down when the royal bee settles down, so it is with speech, mind, sight and hearing. Pleased, they praised the life-breath:

5.
"He burns as fire. He is the sun.
He is the rain cloud. He is the bountiful.[7] He is the wind.
He is earth, matter, power of nature (*deva*),
being and nonbeing, and what is immortal.[8]

6.

"Like spokes on the hub of a wheel,
everything is established in the life-breath—
Ṛik, Yajus and Sāma,
yagya, kshatriya and *brāhmaṇa*.[9]

7.

"It is you who move in the womb as lord of creation;
it is you alone who are born anew.
All creatures bring you sustenance,
O life-breath, who dwell with the senses.

8.

"You are the chief bearer [of offerings] to the gods;
you are the first offering to the fathers;
you are the true way of the seers,[10]
descendants of Atharvan and Angiras.

9.

"Through your brilliance, O life-breath, you are Indra,
as the protector of all, you are Rudra,
as the sun, you move through the firmament,
you, the lord of lights.

10.

"When you send down rain, O life-breath,
then these your creatures
live in happiness, thinking,
'There will be food as we desire.'

11.
"You are pure by nature, O life-breath,
the lone seer, the devourer, the lord of all that is.
It is we who offer you food.
You are our father, O Mātarishvan.[11]

12.
"Your form, which is lodged in speech,
in hearing and in sight,
and which pervades the mind—
make it benign. Do not leave us.

13.
"All that is here and all that is in the third heaven
falls under the dominion of the life-breath.
Protect us, as a mother her children.
Grant us affluence and a clear understanding."

Third Prashna

1.
Then Kausalya, son of Ashvala, asked him, "Revered Sir, from where does this life-breath (*prāṇa*) arise? How does it enter this body? Having divided itself, how does it dwell there? How does it depart? How is it linked to the outer world, how to the inner?"

2.
He answered him, "You ask questions beyond the ordinary. Since you are greatly devoted to Brahman, I will tell you.

3.
"This life-breath is born of the Self. Just as a shadow spreads over a man, so does the life-breath spread over the Self. Through the activity of the mind, it enters the body.

4.
"As the king orders his officials, telling them, 'You govern these villages and you govern those villages,' so does this life-breath direct the other breaths, one by one.

5.
"The downward breath (*apāna*) resides in the organs of excretion and reproduction. The life-breath itself (*prāṇa*), passing through the mouth and nose, resides in the eyes and ears. And the even breath (*samāna*) resides in the middle, for it makes even what has been offered as food. From the even breath arise these seven flames.[12]

6.
"This Self surely lives in the heart. Here there are a hundred and one channels.[13] Each of these divides into a hundred channels, and each of them into seventy-two thousand branching channels. Among them stirs the pervading breath (*vyāna*).

7.
"Now the upward breath (*udāna*), rising through one of these channels, leads by way of good deeds to a world of good, by way of evil deeds to a world of evil and by way of both together to the world of men.

8.

"The sun surely rises as the external life-breath, since it cares for the life-breath in the eye. The deity (*devatā*) which is in the earth sustains a person's downward breath. The space which is between [sun and earth] is the even breath. Air is the pervading breath.

9.

"Light surely is the upward breath. Therefore, he whose light has gone out is reborn, his senses absorbed in his mind.

10.

"Whatever his state of mind [at the time of death], with that he enters the life-breath. The life-breath united with the upward breath,[14] together with the Self, leads him to the kind of world he desires.

11.

"When a man of wisdom thus knows the life-breath, his line of offspring is not broken. He becomes immortal. Regarding it there is this verse:

12.

"Knowing the source, entry, dwelling[15]
and the fivefold display of the life-breath
in relation to the body, one gains immortality;
knowing this, one gains immortality."

Fourth Prashna

1.

Then Gārgya, grandson of Sūrya, asked him, "Revered Sir, who are they that sleep in a person here? Who are they that are awake in him? Who is the deity (*deva*) that sees dreams? Who experiences this happiness? In whom are all these joined together?"

2.

He answered him, "O Gārgya, as the rays of the setting sun become united in that circle of radiance, and as they spread out each time it rises, even so does everything here become united in the highest deity, the mind. So at that time a person hears not, sees not, smells not, tastes not, feels not, speaks not, grasps nothing, enjoys no pleasure, discharges not, moves not. People say, 'He is asleep.'

3.

"Only the fires of life remain awake in this city.[16] The downward breath (*apāna*) is the householder fire. The pervading breath (*vyāna*) is the southern fire. The life-breath (*prāṇa*) is the oblation fire, since it is taken out (*praṇayana*)—taken (*praṇīyate*) from the householder's fire.

4.

"The even breath (*samāna*) is so named because it brings evenness (*sama*) between the two offerings, the in-breath and the out-breath. The mind, indeed, is the patron of the sacrifice (*yajamāna*). The desired fruit is the upward breath (*udāna*). Day after day it leads the patron of the sacrifice to Brahman.

5.
"There, in his dreams, this deity experiences greatness. He sees again what was seen before, he hears again what was heard before. Time after time he experiences what he experienced in different places and regions of the world: the seen and the unseen, the heard and the unheard, what has been experienced and what has not been experienced, the real and the unreal. He sees everything; he is everything he sees.

6.
"When he is overwhelmed by radiance, that deity sees no dreams. Then in this body there arises happiness.

7.
"As birds, dear friend, flock to a tree for shelter, so do all things resort to the supreme Self:

8.
"earth and the [subtle] element of earth, water and the element of water, fire and the element of fire, air and the element of air, space and the element of space, sight and what can be seen, hearing and what can be heard, smell and what can be smelled, taste and what can be tasted, touch and what can be touched, speech and what can be spoken, the hands and what can be held, the organ of generation and what can be enjoyed, the anus and what can be excreted, the feet and what can be walked upon, the mind and what can be thought, the intellect and what can be chosen, the ego and what can be experienced, awareness and what can be known, light and what can be lit up, the life-breath and what can be held together by it.

9.
"It is he alone who sees, touches, hears, smells, tastes, thinks, knows, acts—the intelligent Self, Purusha. He is fully established in the highest, indestructible Self.

10.
"He alone attains the highest imperishable who knows the imperishable—shadowless, bodiless, qualityless, pure. He, dear friend, knowing all, is all. Regarding it there is this verse:

11.
"Dear friend, he who knows that imperishable,
in which are established the intelligent Self,
with all its powers (*deva*), and the vital breaths
and the elements—he, knowing all, has entered all."

Fifth Prashna

1.
Then Satyakāma, son of Shibi, asked him, "Revered Sir, if someone in the world of men becomes absorbed in the sound *Om* until his last moment, what world will he win by that?"

2.
He answered him, "Satyakāma, that which is the sound *Om* is indeed both the higher (*para*) and the lower (*apara*) Brahman.[17] Therefore the wise man by this same means attains one or the other.

3.
"If he becomes absorbed in one letter (*a*),[18] he gains knowledge by that alone. Very soon he comes back to this world. The Ṛik verses guide him to the world of men, where, endowed with austerity, celibacy and faith, he experiences greatness.

4.
"Now, if he becomes absorbed in two letters (*a, u*), he is united with mind. He is guided by the Yajus formulas to the intermediate region, the world of *soma* [the moon]. After experiencing glory in the lunar world, he returns again.

5.
"However he who becomes absorbed in the supreme Purusha by the three letters (*a, u, m*) of the syllable *Om*, is united with the brilliance in the sun. As a serpent is freed from its skin, just so is he set free from sin. He is guided by the Sāma chants to the world of Brahmā. From this totality of living beings,[19] he sees Purusha, higher than the highest, dwelling in the city of the body. Regarding it there are these two verses:

6.
"The three parts fall within the orbit of death.
But when they are joined to one another, not used separately,
when they are used in actions well-performed—external,
internal, or in-between[20]—the knower does not tremble.

7.
"This world [is attained] with the Ṛik verses;
the intermediate region, with the Yajus formulas;
that [world of Brahmā] which the sages know,
with the Sāma chants.
Just with the sound *Om* as his support, the wise man attains
what is tranquil, beyond old age and death,
free from fear—the supreme."

Sixth Prashna

1.
Then Sukeshā, son of Bharadvāja, asked him, "Revered Sir, Hiraṇyanābha, a prince of Kosala, came to me and asked this question, 'Bhāradvāja,[21] do you know the Purusha with sixteen parts?' I told that young prince, 'I do not know him. If I had known him, why would I not have told you? He who speaks untruth shrivels up to his very roots. Therefore, I cannot speak untruth.' Silently he mounted his chariot and went away.

"So I ask this of you, 'Where is that Purusha?'"

2.
Then he answered him, "Here, within this very body, gentle friend, is that Purusha in whom arise these sixteen parts.[22]

3.
"He [Purusha] reflected, 'Who is it that goes when I go and stays when I stay?'

4.
"He brought forth the life-breath (*prāṇa*); from the life-breath came faith, space, air, light, water, earth, the senses, mind and food; from food came vigor, self-control (*tapas*), the *mantras,*[23] the rites, the worlds,[24] and in the worlds, name.[25]

5.
"Just as these flowing rivers heading toward the ocean disappear once they have reached it, their name and form shattered, and people just speak of the ocean—even so the sixteen parts of the seer heading toward Purusha disappear once they have reached him, their name and form shattered, and people just speak of Purusha. Then he is freed from parts, immortal. Regarding it there is this verse:

6.
"He in whom the parts find their rest,
like spokes on the hub of a wheel—
know him, the Purusha, worthy to be known,
so that death may not disquiet you."

7.
Then Pippalāda said to them, "This is what I know about the supreme Brahman. Beyond this there is nothing."

8.
They honored him and said, "Truly you are our father, who takes us beyond ignorance to the other shore."

Homage to the great seers.
Homage to the great seers.

All good I should hear from the ears, O radiant beings.
All good I should see through the eyes, O revered ones.
May we, full of praise, with bodies firm of limb,
enjoy the span of life given us by God.

May Indra, swelling in glory, grant us well-being.
May Pūshan, who knows all, grant us well-being.
May Tārkshya, who saves from harm, grant us well-being.
May Bṛihaspati confer upon us well-being.
Oṁ shāntiḥ shāntiḥ shāntiḥ

Muṇḍaka Upanishad[1]

All good I should hear from the ears, O radiant beings.
All good I should see through the eyes, O revered ones.
May we, full of praise, with bodies firm of limb,
enjoy the span of life given us by God.

May Indra, swelling in glory, grant us well-being.
May Pūshan, who knows all, grant us well-being.
May Tārkshya, who saves from harm, grant us well-being.
May Bṛihaspati confer upon us well-being.
Oṁ shāntiḥ shāntiḥ shāntiḥ

First Muṇḍaka

First Khaṇḍa

1.
Brahmā arose first among the *devas*,
the creator of all, the guardian of the world.

He taught the knowledge of Brahman (*brahma vidyā*),
the basis of all knowledge, to Atharvaṇ, his firstborn son.[2]

2.
The knowledge of Brahman, which Brahmā spoke out
to Atharvaṇ, Atharvaṇ taught to Angir in ancient times.
Angir taught it to Satyavāha, the son of Bhāradvāja.
Satyavāha taught it to Angiras—from the earlier to the later.

3.
Shaunaka, a great householder, once approached Angiras in the prescribed manner and asked, "My lord, what is that, knowing which, everything becomes known?"

4.
Angiras then said to him, "Two kinds of knowledge are to be gained, as indeed the knowers of Brahman declare—higher (*parā*) and also lower (*aparā*)."

5.
Of these, the lower consists of the Ṛig Veda, Yajur Veda, Sāma Veda, Atharva Veda, science of expression (Shikshā), rules for Vedic ritual (Kalpa), grammar (Vyākaraṇa), etymology (Nirukta), meter (Chandas) and Vedic astrology (Jyotisha).

The higher is that by which the imperishable is known.

6.
That which is beyond sight, beyond grasp, without source,
without features, without eyes or ears, without hands or feet,

eternal, all-pervading, omnipresent, extremely subtle—that is the imperishable, which the wise know as the womb of beings.

7.
As a spider spins out and draws in its threads,
as herbs sprout from the earth,
as hair grows from the head and body of a living person,
so does this world spring from the imperishable.

8.
Through the power of meditation,
Brahman swells. From that, food is born.
From food arises life (*prāṇa*), then mind, the elements,
the worlds and, through action, immortality.

9.
He who is all-knowing, all-wise,
whose austerity consists of knowledge,
from him are born this Brahmā,
name, form and food.

Second Khaṇḍa

1.
This is the truth. The rites which the seers cognized
in the hymns (*mantra*) are spread variously across the three
Vedas. Perform them always, you who seek truth.
This is your path to the world of good deeds.

2.
When the flame shoots up,
after the fire is kindled,
then should one make offerings
between the two portions of ghee.[3]

3.
When the daily fire offering (*agnihotra*) is made
without the new-moon, full-moon and four-month rite,
without the harvest oblation, without inviting guests,
or without any oblations at all,
when it is not offered to all the gods or not according to rule,
then it ruins one's future in the worlds, up to the seventh.

4.
The black, the terrible, the swift-as-mind,
the red, the smoke-colored,
the sparkling and the all-gleaming *devī*—[4]
these are the seven flickering tongues of fire.

5.
When one offers oblations into these flames
as they shine bright and makes them at the right time,
then the flames, becoming rays of the sun, lead him
to the place where the one lord of the gods resides.

6.
Saying "Come, come," the shining oblations
carry the patron of the sacrifice along the sun's rays,

calling out, praising him with endearing words,[5]
"This is yours, the fair world of Brahmā, won by good deeds."

7.
Alas, these rafts are frail,
these eighteen elements of ritual, on which
the lesser activity is said to rest. Fools who hail
this as best, return yet again to aging and death.[6]

8.
Living in the midst of ignorance,
wise in their own eyes, thinking themselves scholars,
fools go round and round, beset by troubles,
like the blind led by the blind.[7]

9.
Such children, living in every kind of ignorance,
think, "We have achieved our goals." But these offerers,
swayed by attachment, not knowing the truth,
sink down, desolate, when their worlds collapse.

10.
Thinking the merit from sacred rites and charitable works
as supreme, these foolish men know nothing better.
After enjoying the heights of heaven through their good deeds,
they enter this world or a lower one.

11.
But those men, tranquil and wise, who lead a life
of self-control and faith in the forest, collecting alms,
free from impurity, go by the gateway of the sun
to where dwells that immortal Purusha, that undecaying Self.

12.
When he has considered the worlds won by deeds,
let a Brāhmaṇa gain nonattachment. What is not made
cannot be won by what is made. For that knowledge,
let him, sacrificial firewood in hand, approach a master
versed in the Veda and established in Brahman.

13.
To that pupil of peaceful mind and calm senses, who has
approached him in the proper way, the enlightened one
should fully impart that knowledge of Brahman, by which
one knows the Purusha, the imperishable, the true.

Second Muṇḍaka

First Khaṇḍa

1.
This is the truth:
As from a blazing fire a thousand sparks
of like nature leap forth,
so, my gentle friend, beings of many kinds spring up
from the indestructible (*akshara*) and return there also.

2.
Resplendent is Purusha, without form.
He is without and within, unborn,
without breath, without mind. Shining,
he is beyond the highest indestructible (*akshara*).[8]

3.
From him are born life,
mind and all the senses,
also space, air, light, water
and earth, the bearer of all.

4.
His head is fire, his eyes are the moon and the sun, his ears
are the regions of space, his speech is the Vedas unfolded,
his breath is the wind, his heart is the universe and from his
feet comes the earth. Truly, he is the inner Self of all beings.

5.
From him comes fire, whose fuel is the sun.
From the moon comes the raincloud, and [from rain]
plants grow on earth. Man pours seed into woman.
From Purusha many creatures are born.

6.
From him are the Vedic utterances—Ṛik, Sāma and Yajus—
the initial dedication, and all the *yagyas*,[9] the rites
and sacrificial gifts, the time of the ceremony,

the patron of the *yagya* and the [meritorious] worlds[10]
where the moon purifies and where the sun [shines].

7.
And from him are born *devas* in various groups,
sādhyas,[11] humans, beasts and birds,
the in-breath and the out-breath, rice and barley,
self-control, faith, truth, chastity and law.

8.
From him come forth the seven life-breaths, the seven flames, their fuel, the seven offerings; also the seven worlds in which move the life-breaths that are hidden in the cave of the heart, placed in groups of seven.[12]

9.
From him come all seas and mountains,
from him flow rivers of every kind,
and from him are all plants and the sap
whereby the inner Self dwells among the elements.

10.
Purusha alone is all this—action and knowledge.
He who knows this Brahman, the supreme, the immortal,
set in the cave of the heart, my gentle friend,
cuts the knot of ignorance in this very life.

Second Khaṇḍa

1\.
Luminous, near at hand, known as moving in the cave
of the heart, that is the great goal. All that stirs,
breathes and blinks is found within it. Know that as
what is and what is not,[13] beyond the understanding
of creatures, most charming, highest of all.

2\.
That which is radiant, subtler than the subtle, in which rest
the worlds and those in the worlds—that is the imperishable
Brahman. That is life. That is speech and mind. That is
the true. That is the immortal. That is to be pierced.
Pierce it, my gentle friend!

3\.
Taking as your bow the mighty weapon, the Upanishad,
fix on it the arrow made sharp by meditation.
Drawing it back, your mind going to the essence of that,
hit the target—that imperishable—my friend.

4\.
The sacred syllable is the bow, the Self is the arrow,
Brahman is declared the target.
Undistracted, one should pierce it,
and like the arrow, become united with it.

5.
He on whom are woven sky, earth and the space between,
also mind, along with all the vital organs—
know him alone as the one Self.
Banish other talk. This is the bridge to immortality.

6.
Where the arteries are joined together like spokes on the hub of a chariot wheel, there he stirs within [himself], becoming manifold. That is *Om.* Recollect the Self thus. May it be well with you as you move beyond darkness to the further shore.

7.
He who is all-knowing, all-wise,
whose is the glory here on earth—
he is this Self, seated in the space [within the heart],[14]
the shining city of Brahman.

8.
Filling the mind, the guide of life-breath and body,
the Self is established in food [the body], having settled
in the heart. By means of this knowledge the wise realize
the immortal Self, shining, full of bliss.

9.
The knot of the heart is severed,
all doubts are dispelled,
and one's accumulated deeds (*karmāṇi*) are destroyed
when he is seen as beyond the world and in it.

10.

Within the veil made of gold[15] is Brahman,
stainless, without parts.
That is the pure, the light of lights,
that is what knowers of the Self know.

11.

There the sun shines not, nor the moon nor stars,
nor do these lightnings shine, much less this fire.
Only when he shines does everything shine.
This whole world shines by his light.[16]

12.

Brahman, truly, is this immortal.
Brahman is in front, Brahman is behind,
it is to the right and to the left, it extends below and above.
This whole world is nothing but Brahman, the supreme.

Third Muṇḍaka

First Khaṇḍa

1.

Two birds, closely bound by friendship,
cling to the same tree.
One of them eats the *pippala* berry,
the other looks on without eating.[17]

2.

On the very same tree a person, drowned [in ignorance],
suffers out of helplessness, completely bewildered.

When he sees the other, the adorable lord,
and sees his greatness, he is freed from sorrow.

3.
When the seer sees Purusha, the golden-hued,
the creator, the lord, the source of Brahmā,
then that man of wisdom, having shaken off good and evil,
free from stain, attains perfect unity.

4.
Truly this is the life that shines in many ways through all
beings. Knowing this, the wise man speaks of nothing more.
Playful in the Self, delighting in the Self, doing right action,
he is greatest among the knowers of Brahman.

5.
This Self is attained through the constant practice of truth,
meditation, right knowledge and a chaste life.
Their blemishes destroyed, the enlightened (*yati*) perceive him,
made only of light, resplendent, dwelling within the body.

6.
Truth alone triumphs,[18] never nontruth.
The path to the divine is paved with truth;
along it the seers, their desires satisfied,
approach truth's highest dwelling.

7.
Vast, divine, of inconceivable form, subtler than
the subtle, that shines forth, farther than the farthest,

and yet here, near at hand.[19] It is here within those
who see, set in the secret place of the heart.

8.
Not by the eye is it grasped, nor even by speech, nor by
the other senses, nor by austerity or action. When one's
nature is purified by the clarity of knowledge, only then,
as he meditates, does he perceive him, the indivisible.

9.
This subtle Self is to be known through pure intelligence
into which the life-breath has entered in its fivefold form.
The whole of man's thought is entwined with his life-breaths.
When thought is purified, this Self shines forth.

10.
Whatever world a man of purified nature sees clearly
in his mind, and whatever desires he desires,
that world and those desires he wins. Therefore he who
desires well-being should honor him who knows the Self.

Second Khaṇḍa

1.
He knows that highest dwelling, that Brahman.
This whole world, resting on that, shines brightly.
The wise, free from desires, who serve Purusha,
pass beyond the seed [of rebirth].

2.
He who forms desires, brooding on them,
is born in this and that place still carrying his desires.[20]
But for one whose desire is satisfied, who is perfected
in the Self, all desires are dissolved even here on earth.

3.
This Self cannot be gained by instruction,
nor by the intellect, nor yet by much learning.[21]
He is gained only by one whom he chooses.
To him, this Self reveals his own nature.

4.
This Self cannot be gained by one who is weak or lazy,
nor by meditative practice that is faulty.
But for that man of wisdom who proceeds by proper means,[22]
the Self enters the dwelling of Brahman.

5.
Having fully attained him, the seers are content in knowledge,
perfected in the Self, freed from passion, tranquil.
On realizing the all-pervading one everywhere,
those wise men, in union with the Self, enter into the all.

6.
Those who have fully understood the goal of Vedānta
wisdom, who have persevered in the yoga of renunciation
and have purified their nature—all these, the highest
immortals, are fully liberated in the worlds of Brahmā
at the moment of final departure.[23]

7.
The fifteen parts[24] have gone to their sources,
and all the senses to their respective divinities.
One's deeds and the self consisting of intellect
all become one in the supreme immutable being.[25]

8.
As flowing rivers disappear
into the ocean, losing name and form,
so the wise man, freed from name and form,
attains the shining Purusha, higher than the high.[26]

9.
He who knows that highest Brahman becomes that very Brahman itself.[27] No one is born in his family who does not know Brahman. He passes beyond sorrow. He passes beyond evil. Freed from the knots of the heart, he becomes immortal.

10.
It has been said in the Vedic verse:

One may speak this knowledge of Brahman only to those
who perform the rites, who know the Vedas, who are intent
on Brahman, who, possessing faith, offer oblations to the fire
known as the "lone seer,"[28] and who have performed the rite
of carrying fire on the head, according to rule.

11.
This is the truth spoken of old by the seer Angiras. One who has not observed the head-vow does not read this.[29]

Homage to the great seers.
Homage to the great seers.

All good I should hear from the ears, O radiant beings.
All good I should see through the eyes, O revered ones.
May we, full of praise, with bodies firm of limb,
enjoy the span of life given us by God.

May Indra, swelling in glory, grant us well-being.
May Pūshan, who knows all, grant us well-being.
May Tārkshya, who saves from harm, grant us well-being.
May Bṛihaspati confer upon us well-being.
Oṁ shāntiḥ shāntiḥ shāntiḥ

Māṇḍūkya Upanishad[1]

All good I should hear from the ears, O radiant beings.
All good I should see through the eyes, O revered ones.
May we, full of praise, with bodies firm of limb,
enjoy the span of life given us by God.

May Indra, swelling in glory, grant us well-being.
May Pūshan, who knows all, grant us well-being.
May Tārkshya, who saves from harm, grant us well-being.
May Bṛihaspati confer upon us well-being.
Oṁ shāntiḥ shāntiḥ shāntiḥ

1.
Om—this syllable is all there is. A further explanation of it is this: All that is past, present and future is just the sound *Om*. And whatever is beyond the three divisions of time, that is also just the sound *Om*.

2.
Truly, all this is Brahman. This Self is Brahman.[2] This Self has four quarters.

3.
The waking state (*jāgarita-sthāna*) is outwardly cognitive, has seven limbs and nineteen mouths, and enjoys material objects. This first quarter is common to all beings (*vaishvānaraḥ*).

4.
The dreaming state (*svapna-sthāna*) is inwardly cognitive, has seven limbs and nineteen mouths, and enjoys refined objects. This second quarter consists of luminosity (*taijasa*).

5.
When the sleeper desires no desire and sees no dream, that is deep sleep. The deep sleep state (*sushupta-sthāna*) is unified, a mass of intelligence only, consists of bliss and enjoys bliss, and is the gateway to cognition. This third quarter consists of intelligence (*prāgya*).

6.
This is the lord of all. This is the knower of all. This is the inner ruler. This is the womb of all, indeed it is the beginning and end of beings.

7.
That which is not inwardly cognitive, not outwardly cognitive, not cognitive both ways, not a mass of intelligence, neither intelligent nor nonintelligent, unseen, unrelated to anything, un-

graspable, without distinguishing marks, inconceivable, indescribable, the essence of the knowledge of the one Self, the state where manifestation ceases, peaceful, benign, undivided—that is known as the fourth. That is the Self. That is to be realized.

8.
This same Self is the sound *Om*, from the standpoint of the syllable. Taken as letters, the letters of *Om* are the quarters of the Self, and the quarters of the Self are the letters of *Om*, namely *a*, *u* and *m* (*aum*).[3]

9.
The waking state, common to all beings, is *a*, the first letter, because of "pervasiveness" (*āpti*), or because of "being first" (*ādimattva*). He who knows this, does indeed obtain all his desires and becomes the first.

10.
The dreaming state, which consists of luminosity, is *u*, the second letter, because of "excellence" (*utkarsha*) or because of "being in the middle" (*ubhayatva*). He who knows this, does indeed increase his flow of knowledge and becomes the equal of all. In his family no one is born who does not know Brahman.

11.
The sleeping state, which consists of intelligence, is *m*, the third letter, because of "measuring" (*miti*) or because of "absorbing" (*apīti*). He who knows this does indeed measure and absorb all.

12.
The fourth has no parts and is unrelated to anything, the state where manifestation ceases, benign, undivided. Thus the sound *Om* is indeed the Self. He who knows this enters into the Self by the Self. Yes, he who knows this.

All good I should hear from the ears, O radiant beings.
All good I should see through the eyes, O revered ones.
May we, full of praise, with bodies firm of limb,
enjoy the span of life given us by God.

May Indra, swelling in glory, grant us well-being.
May Pūshan, who knows all, grant us well-being.
May Tārkshya, who saves from harm, grant us well-being.
May Bṛihaspati confer upon us well-being.
Oṁ shāntiḥ shāntiḥ shāntiḥ

Taittirīya Upanishad[1]

Shikshā Vallī

First Anuvāka

May Mitra bring us good fortune.
May Varuṇa bring us good fortune.
May Aryaman bring us good fortune.
May Indra and Bṛihaspati bring us good fortune.
May Vishṇu of wide strides bring us good fortune.

I give honor to Brahman.
I give honor to you, O Vāyu.[2]
You are indeed Brahman manifest.
Of you, the manifest Brahman, I will speak.

I will speak what is right.
I will speak what is true.
May that protect me.

May that protect the speaker.
May it protect me.
May it protect the speaker.
Oṁ shāntiḥ shāntiḥ shāntiḥ

Second Anuvāka

We will explain phonetics: sound, accent, length, strength, articulation and sequence. Thus the lesson on phonetics has been declared.

Third Anuvāka

1.

Let us attain fame together. Let us together attain the splendor of Brahman.

Now we will explain the secret knowledge of connection under five headings as they relate to worlds, to lights, to knowledge, to offspring, to the body. They call these the great conjunctions.

As to the worlds, the earth is the prior sound; heaven is the latter sound; space, their junction; air, their link. Thus regarding the worlds.

2.

As to the lights, fire is the prior sound; the sun is the latter sound; water, their junction; lightning, their link. Thus regarding the lights.

3.
As to knowledge, the teacher is the prior sound; the student is the latter sound; knowledge, their junction; instruction, their link. Thus regarding knowledge.

4.
As to offspring, the mother is the prior sound; the father is the latter sound; offspring, their junction; begetting, their link. Thus regarding offspring.

5.
As to the body, the lower jaw is the prior sound; the upper jaw is the latter sound; speech, their junction; the tongue, their link. Thus regarding the body.

6.
These are the great conjunctions. He who knows these great conjunctions, thus explained, is endowed with offspring, with cattle, with the splendor of Brahman, with food to eat and with a heavenly world.

FOURTH ANUVĀKA

1.
May he who is the most excellent in the Vedic hymns,
who is all forms, who has sprung into being from the
immortal hymns, may that Indra endow me with wisdom.
O Lord, may I be the bearer of immortality.

May my body be filled with vigor.
May my tongue be most sweet.
May I hear far and wide with my ears.

You are the sheath of Brahman,
covered by intelligence.
Guard what I have heard.

2.
May fortune (Shrī) bring for me in increasing measure
and without delay clothing and cattle,
food and drink for all time; so bring me then prosperity,
rich in wool and cattle. Hail! (*Svāhā*)

May students of sacred knowledge come to me
 from every side. *Svāhā*.
May students of sacred knowledge come to me
 in different ways. *Svāhā*.
May students of sacred knowledge come to me
 in the right manner. *Svāhā*.
May students of sacred knowledge come to me
 controlled in body. *Svāhā*.
May students of sacred knowledge come to me
 tranquil in mind. *Svāhā*.

3.
May I attain renown among men. *Svāhā*.
May I become more famous than the most wealthy. *Svāhā*.
Into you yourself, O Gracious Lord, may I enter. *Svāhā*.

Do you yourself, O Gracious Lord, enter into me. *Svāhā.*
In you, O Gracious Lord, the thousand branched,
am I cleansed. *Svāhā.*

As waters flow downward, as months flow into the year,
so may students of sacred knowledge come to me
from every side, O dispenser of all things. *Svāhā.*
You are my refuge. Reveal yourself to me! Make me your own!

FIFTH ANUVĀKA

1.

Bhūḥ, bhuvaḥ, suvaḥ—these are the three great utterances. Beside these, the son of Mahāchamasa made known a fourth, *mahaḥ.*[3] That is wholeness (Brahman). That is the Self (*Ātmā*). Other divinities are its limbs.

Bhūḥ then is this world. *Bhuvaḥ* is intermediate space. *Suvaḥ* is the other world. *Mahaḥ* is the sun. By the sun all these worlds flourish.

2.

Bhūḥ then is fire. *Bhuvaḥ* is air. *Suvaḥ* is the sun. *Mahaḥ* is the moon. By the moon all these luminaries flourish.

3.

Bhūḥ then is the Ṛik verses. *Bhuvaḥ* is the Sāma chants. *Suvaḥ* is the Yajus formulas. *Mahaḥ* is Brahman. By Brahman all these Vedas flourish.

4.
Bhūḥ then is the life-breath (*prāṇa*). *Bhuvaḥ* is the downward breath (*apāna*). *Suvaḥ* is the pervading breath (*vyāna*). *Mahaḥ* is food. By food all these vital breaths flourish.

5.
These four groups each have four parts. The utterances are four by four. He who knows them knows Brahman, and to him all the *deva*s bring offerings.

Sixth Anuvāka

1.
There is a space within the heart. Within it dwells Purusha,[4] made of mind, immortal, golden. That which hangs down between two sides of the palate like a nipple, that is along the pathway of Indra (the soul).[5] It pierces the two halves of the skull, passing out at the crown of the head where the hair ends.[6] With the sound *bhūḥ* he is established in fire, with *bhuvaḥ* in air,

2.
with *suvaḥ* in the sun, with *mahaḥ* in Brahman. He obtains self-rule and becomes the lord of the mind, the lord of speech, the lord of sight, the lord of hearing, the lord of understanding. And thereafter he is Brahman, with space his body, truth his soul, life-breath his play, mind his bliss. He flourishes in peace. He is immortal. On that you should reflect, O Prāchīnayogya.

Seventh Anuvāka

1.

Earth, intermediate space, sky, primary directions,
intermediate directions,
fire, air, sun, moon, constellations,
water, herbs, trees, space, body—
thus with respect to material existence (*adhibhūta*).

Now with respect to the self (*adhyātma*):
the life-breath, diffused breath, downward breath,
upward breath, even breath,
sight, hearing, mind, speech, touch,
skin, flesh, muscle, bone, bone marrow.

After grouping them in this way, the seer said, "All this is surely fivefold. Through the fivefold, surely one gains the fivefold."[7]

Eighth Anuvāka

1.

Om is Brahman.[8] *Om* is all this. *Om* is well known as a sign of agreeing to begin. So when they make them recite [with the word *Om*], then they begin the recitation. With *Om* they sing the Sāma chants. With *Om shom* they recite the verses [that are not sung]. With *Om* the *adhvaryu* priest gives the response. With *Om* the *brahma* priest gives the eulogy. With *Om* one gives the offering to the fire. With *Om* the Brāhmaṇa, about to recite, thinks, "May I obtain Brahman."[9] Wishing for Brahman, he obtains Brahman.

Ninth Anuvāka

1.

The practice of what is right and also learning
and recitation of the Veda,[10]
truthfulness and also learning and recitation of the Veda,
self-control and also learning and recitation of the Veda,
calmness and also learning and recitation of the Veda,
the sacrificial fires and also learning
and recitation of the Veda,
the fire sacrifice (*agnihotra*) and also learning
and recitation of the Veda,
guests and also learning and recitation of the Veda,
mankind and also learning and recitation of the Veda,
children and also learning and recitation of the Veda,
propagation and also learning and recitation of the Veda,
descendants and also learning and recitation of the Veda.

"Truthfulness," says Satyavachas Rathītara.[11]
"Self-control," says Taponitya Paurushishti.[12]

"Learning and recitation of the Veda alone," says Nāka Maudgalya, "for that indeed is self-control, that indeed is self-control."

Tenth Anuvāka

1.

I am the mover of the tree.[13]
My fame is like a mountaintop.
Exalted, pure, like the fine nectar in the sun,

I am a radiant treasure,
a man of wisdom, soaked in immortality.
Such is Trishanku's teaching upon[14] attaining the Veda.

Eleventh Anuvāka

1.

Having taught him the Veda, the teacher instructs his student:
"Speak the truth.
Follow *dharma*.[15]
Do not neglect your study.
After you have brought your teacher a [parting] gift,
pleasing to him,
do not cut short the line of offspring.[16]

"Do not neglect the truth.
Do not neglect *dharma*.
Do not neglect your health.
Do not neglect your well-being.
Do not neglect learning and recitation of the Veda.
Do not neglect your duties to the gods and to your forefathers.

2.

"Honor your mother as divine.
Honor your father as divine.
Honor your teacher as divine.
Honor your guest as divine.[17]

"Those actions that are without fault,
do those and no others.

Those good actions that are done by your teachers,
do those and no others.

3.
"Those Brāhmaṇas who are more distinguished than us should be made comfortable with a seat.[18]

"You should give with respect.
You should not give without respect.
You should give with abundance.[19]
You should give with modesty.
You should give with care.
You should give with understanding.

4.
"Now, if at any time you have a doubt regarding the performance of rites, any doubt regarding conduct, you should behave as those Brāhmaṇas present behave in such matters—Brāhmaṇas who have good judgment, are experienced, independent, not harsh and who love *dharma*.

"Likewise, regarding persons who are accused without reason, you should behave as those Brāhmaṇas present behave toward such people—Brāhmaṇas who have good judgment, are experienced, independent, not harsh and who love *dharma*.

"This is the injunction.[20]
This is the admonition.[21]
This is the secret knowledge (*upanishad*) of the Veda.
This is the instruction.

This, one should be intent upon.
Yes this, one should be intent upon."

Twelth Anuvāka

May Mitra bring us good fortune.
May Varuṇa bring us good fortune.
May Aryaman bring us good fortune.
May Indra and Bṛihaspati bring us good fortune.
May Vishṇu of wide strides bring us good fortune.

I give honor to Brahman.
I give honor to you, O Vāyu.
You are indeed Brahman manifest.
Of you, the manifest Brahman, I have spoken.

I have spoken what is right.
I have spoken what is true.
That has protected me.
That has protected the speaker.
It has protected me.
It has protected the speaker.
Oṁ shāntiḥ shāntiḥ shāntiḥ

Brahmānanda Vallī

First Anuvāka

Let us be together.
Let us eat together.
Let us be vital together.
Let us be radiating truth,
radiating the light of life.
Never shall we denounce anyone,
never entertain negativity.
Oṁ shāntiḥ shāntiḥ shāntiḥ

Om. The knower of Brahman attains the highest.
Concerning this, it has been declared:

Brahman is truth, knowledge, infinity.
He who knows Brahman dwelling in the secret place,
in the field of the transcendent,
wins all desires together with Brahman, the all-knowing.

From this Self (*Ātmā*) arose space; from space, air; from air, fire; from fire, water; from water, earth; from earth, herbs; from herbs, food; and from food, man.

This, then, is the man that is made from the essence of food. This, indeed, is his head. This is the right wing. This is the left wing. This is his self.[22] This is the tail, which gives stability.[23] As to that, there is the following verse:

Second Anuvāka

From food alone are born
all creatures that rest on earth.
By food alone they live,
and into food they pass in the end.

Food is the firstborn of beings,
and so is called the healing herb of all.
Those who worship Brahman as food,
surely obtain all food.

Food is the eldest of beings,
and so is called the healing herb of all.
From food beings are born.
By food, once born, they flourish.

It eats and it is eaten,
and so is called food.

Different from and placed within the self made of the essence of food is the self made of vital breath, by which the self made of food is filled. The self made of breath also is shaped like a person. Its human form matches the form of the other [the self made of food]. The life-breath (*prāṇa*) is his head. The moving breath (*vyāna*) is his right wing. The downward breath (*apāna*) is his left wing. Space is his self. Earth is his tail, which gives stability. As to that there is the following verse:

Third Anuvāka

Gods, men and animals all breathe,
following the life-breath (*prāṇa*),
for *prāṇa* is the life of beings,
and so is called the life of all.

Those devoted to *prāṇa* as Brahman
attain a full span of life,
for *prāṇa* is the life of beings,
and so is called the life of all.

Different from and placed within the self made of breath is the self made of mind, by which the self made of breath is filled. The self made of mind also is shaped like a person. Its human form matches the form of the other [the self made of breath]. The Yajus is his head. The Ṛik is his right wing. The Sāma is his left wing. Teaching is his self. The hymns of the Atharvans and Angirases[24] are his tail, which gives stability. As to that there is the following verse:

Fourth Anuvāka

That from which speech turns back[25]
along with the mind, which cannot reach it—
he who knows the bliss of Brahman,
fears not ever again.

This is the embodied self of the preceding one [mind]. Different from and placed within the self made of mind is the self made of intelligence, by which the self made of mind is filled. The self made of intelligence also is shaped like a person. Its human form matches the form of the other [the self made of mind]. Faith is his head. The right is his right wing. Truth is his left wing. Yoga is his self. *Mahaḥ*[26] is his tail, which gives stability. As to that there is the following verse:

Fifth Anuvāka

Intelligence accomplishes the sacrifice,
and it accomplishes action as well.
All the gods worship intelligence
as Brahman, the foremost.

If one knows Brahman as intelligence,
and neglects it not,
he leaves behind evils in the body
and fulfills all desires.

This is the embodied self of the preceding one [intelligence]. Different from and placed within the self made of intelligence is the self made of bliss, by which the self made of intelligence is filled. The self made of bliss also is shaped like a person. Its human form matches the form of the other [the self made of intelligence]. Pleasure is his head. Delight is his right wing. Enchantment is his left wing. Bliss is his self. Brahman is his tail, which gives stability. As to that there is the following verse:

Sixth Anuvāka

If a person thinks Brahman does not exist,
then that person becomes unreal.
If a person knows that Brahman exists,
then people know him to be real.[27]

This indeed is the embodied self of the preceding one.
Now the following questions arise:

Does someone who knows not
go to the other world upon departing?
Or does someone who knows
reach the other world upon departing?

He [the Creator] desired, "May I become many.
May I give birth." He went into himself.
Having gone into himself, he created all this, whatever is here.
Having created it, he entered into it.[28]

Having entered into it, he became the formed and the formless,
the expressed and the unexpressed, the fixed
and the nonfixed, the sentient and the nonsentient,
the real[29] and the nonreal.

As the real,[30] he became whatever is here.
So they call that the real.

As to that there is the following verse:

Seventh Anuvāka

In the beginning, all this was not-being.
From that, being was born.
That fashioned itself by itself.
Therefore it is called well made.

That, being well made, is truly the essence.
Surely by grasping the essence, one is filled with bliss.
Who indeed would breathe, who would be alive
if this bliss did not pervade space?[31]
For this essence alone bestows delight.

One is freed from fear
only when he finds that fearless ground—
invisible, bodiless,
unutterable, undefined.

But when he makes even
the smallest breach within it,
then he has fear.[32] That indeed is the fear
of one who thinks he knows.

As to that there is the following verse:

Eighth Anuvāka

From fear of him the wind blows.
From fear of him the sun rises.
From fear they take flight:
Agni and Indra and death, the fifth.[33]

Here is the inquiry concerning bliss:

Let there be a youth, a good youth—
well studied, most nimble, steadfast and strong.
Let this whole earth, filled with wealth, be his.
That is a single measure of bliss for mankind.[34]

That which is a hundred times greater than the bliss
of mankind is a single measure of bliss
for human *gandharvas*,[35] also for a person who
knows the Veda[36] and is not smitten by desire.

That which is a hundred times greater than the bliss
of human *gandharvas* is a single measure of bliss
for celestial *gandharvas*, also for a person who
knows the Veda and is not smitten by desire.

That which is a hundred times greater than the bliss
of celestial *gandharvas* is a single measure of bliss
for the fathers in their long-enduring world, also for a person
who knows the Veda and is not smitten by desire.

That which is a hundred times greater than the bliss
of the fathers in their long-enduring world is a single measure
of bliss for those who are gods by birth, also for a person
who knows the Veda and is not smitten by desire.

That which is a hundred times greater than the bliss
of the gods by birth is a single measure of bliss for those who

became gods through their good deeds, also for a person
who knows the Veda and is not smitten by desire.

That which is a hundred times greater than the bliss
of the gods through good deeds is a single measure of bliss
for the [highest] gods, also for a person who
knows the Veda and is not smitten by desire.

That which is a hundred times greater than the bliss
of the [highest] gods is a single measure of bliss for Indra,
also for a person who knows the Veda
and is not smitten by desire.

That which is a hundred times greater than the bliss
of Indra is a single measure of bliss for Bṛihaspati,
also for a person who knows the Veda
and is not smitten by desire.

That which is a hundred times greater than the bliss
of Bṛihaspati is a single measure of bliss for Prajāpati,
also for a person who knows the Veda
and is not smitten by desire.

That which is a hundred times greater than the bliss
of Prajāpati is a single measure of bliss for Brahmā,
also for a person who knows the Veda
and is not smitten by desire.

He who is here in the person
and he who is there in the sun—he is one.[37]

He who knows this, passing beyond this world,
attains the self which consists of food,
attains to the self which consists of breath,
attains to the self which consists of mind,
attains to the self which consists of intelligence,
attains to the self which consists of bliss.

As to that there is the following verse:

Ninth Anuvāka

That from which speech turns back
along with the mind, which cannot reach it—
he who knows the bliss of Brahman,
fears not at any time.

He does not torment himself, thinking, "Why have I not done what is right? Why have I done what is sinful?" Knowing this [the bliss of Brahman], he frees himself from these thoughts. For he who knows this, indeed frees himself from both of these. Such is the hidden teaching (*upanishad*).

Let us be together.
Let us eat together.
Let us be vital together.
Let us be radiating truth,
radiating the light of life.
Never shall we denounce anyone,
never entertain negativity.
Oṁ shāntiḥ shāntiḥ shāntiḥ

Bhṛigu Vallī

First Anuvāka

Let us be together.
Let us eat together.
Let us be vital together.
Let us be radiating truth,
radiating the light of life.
Never shall we denounce anyone,
never entertain negativity.
Oṁ shāntiḥ shāntiḥ shāntiḥ

Bhṛigu, the son of Varuṇa, approached his father,
Varuṇa, and said, "Sir, teach me Brahman."
His father told him this: "Food, life-breath,
sight, hearing, mind, speech."

Then he said, "That, indeed, from which these beings are born,
that by which, once born, they are sustained,
and that to which they go and merge again.
That, seek to know. That is Brahman."

Bhṛigu went within.
Having gone within,

Second Anuvāka

he recognized that food is Brahman.
For truly, from food these beings are born,
by food they are sustained,
and to food they go and merge again.

Having understood that, he again approached his father,
Varuṇa, and said, "Sir, teach me Brahman."
His father said to him, "Seek to know Brahman
by going within. Brahman is found within."[38]

He went within.
Having gone within,

Third Anuvāka

he recognized that life-breath is Brahman.
For truly, from life-breath these beings are born,
by life-breath they are sustained,
and to life-breath they go and merge again.

Having understood that, he again approached his father,
Varuṇa, and said, "Sir, teach me Brahman."
His father said to him, "Seek to know Brahman
by going within. Brahman is found within."

He went within.
Having gone within,

Fourth Anuvāka

he recognized that mind is Brahman.
For truly, from mind these beings are born,
by mind they are sustained,
and to mind they go and merge again.

Having understood that, he again approached his father,
Varuṇa, and said, "Sir, teach me Brahman."
His father said to him, "Seek to know Brahman
by going within. Brahman is found within."

He went within.
Having gone within,

Fifth Anuvāka

he recognized that intelligence is Brahman.
For truly, from intelligence these beings are born,
by intelligence they are sustained,
and to intelligence they go and merge again.

Having recognized that, he again approached his father,
Varuṇa, and said, "Sir, teach me Brahman."
His father said to him, "Seek to know Brahman
by going within. Brahman is found within."

He went within.
Having gone within,

Sixth Anuvāka

he recognized that bliss is Brahman.
For truly, out of bliss these beings are born,
in bliss they are sustained,
and to bliss they go and merge again.[39]

This is the wisdom of Bhṛigu, son of Varuṇa.
It is found in the transcendental field.
One who knows this becomes steadfast.

Rich in food, he eats food.[40]
He becomes great in offspring and cattle,
great in the radiance of Brahman.
He becomes great in fame.[41]

Seventh Anuvāka

One should not disparage food. That is the rule.
Life-breath, indeed, is food. The body is the eater of food.
The body is established in life-breath; life-breath is
established in the body. Thus food is established in food.

He who knows that food is established in food,
becomes steadfast. Rich in food, he eats food.
He becomes great in offspring and cattle, great in
the radiance of Brahman. He becomes great in fame.

Eighth Anuvāka

One should not reject food. That is the rule.
Water, indeed, is food. Fire is the eater of food.
Fire is established in water; water is established in fire.
Thus food is established in food.

He who knows that food is established in food,
becomes steadfast. Rich in food, he eats food.
He becomes great in offspring and cattle, great in
the radiance of Brahman. He becomes great in fame.

Ninth Anuvāka

One should prepare an abundance of food. That is the rule.
Earth, indeed, is food. Space is the eater of food.
Space is established in earth; earth is established in space.
Thus food is established in food.

He who knows that food is established in food,
becomes steadfast. Rich in food, he eats food.
He becomes great in offspring and cattle, great in
the radiance of Brahman. He becomes great in fame.

Tenth Anuvāka

1.

One should not turn anyone away from one's home.
That is the rule. Therefore, one should obtain
an abundance of food by every possible means.
Then people will say, "Food is prepared for him [the guest]."

Food that is prepared in the best manner
returns to the giver in the best manner.
Food that is prepared in a medium manner
returns to the giver in a medium manner.

Food that is prepared in the worst manner
returns to the giver in the worst manner.

2.

He who knows this [obtains what he deserves].

[He knows Brahman] as ease in speech;
as rest and activity in the in-breath and out-breath;
as action in the hands, movement in the feet, evacuation
in the anus—this is knowledge pertaining to mankind.

Now pertaining to the cosmos—
[Brahman is seen as] satisfaction in rain,
as power in lightning,

3.

as splendor in beasts, as light in heavenly bodies,
as procreation, immortality and bliss in the generative organ,
as the wholeness of space.

One should revere that as the steadfast;
then he becomes steadfast.
One should revere that as the great;
then he becomes great.

One should revere that as the mind;
then he becomes mindful.

4.

One should revere that as homage;
then his desires bow down to him.
One should revere that as Brahman;
then he becomes Brahman.

One should revere that as the means of destruction
from all around, belonging to Brahman;
then his adversaries, full of hate,
and those kinsmen he dislikes will perish all around him.

He who is here in the person
and he who is there in the sun—he is one.

5.
He who knows this, passing beyond this world,
steps on to the self which consists of food,
steps on to the self which consists of breath,
steps on to the self which consists of mind,
steps on to the self which consists of intelligence,
steps on to the self which consists of bliss.

Crossing these worlds,
eating the food he desires,
assuming the forms he desires,
he continues singing this song of praise:

Oh, wonderful!
Oh, wonderful!
Oh, wonderful!
(*hā vu hā vu hā vu*)

6.
I am food! I am food! I am food!
I am the food eater! I am the food eater! I am the food eater!
I am the unifier! I am the unifier! I am the unifier!

I am the firstborn of the cosmic order, earlier than the gods,
the navel of immortality.

He who gives me away, protects me.
I who am food eat up him who eats food.
I have overcome the whole universe.
I am golden like the sun.

And so it is for him who knows this.
Thus the Upanishad.

Let us be together.
Let us eat together.
Let us be vital together.
Let us be radiating truth,
radiating the light of life.
Never shall we denounce anyone,
never entertain negativity.
Oṁ shāntiḥ shāntiḥ shāntiḥ

Aitareya Upanishad[1]

May my speech rest on my mind.
May my mind rest on my speech.
O manifest one, be manifest to me.
May both mind and speech secure the Veda for me.
May all that I have heard not depart from me.
By this study I shall bring together day and night.

I will speak what is right.
I will speak what is true.
May that protect me.
May that protect the speaker.
May it protect me.
May it protect the speaker.
May it protect the speaker.
Oṁ shāntiḥ shāntiḥ shāntiḥ

FIRST ADHYĀYA

FIRST KHAṆDA

1.

In the beginning, the Self (*Ātmā*) alone was here. Nothing else blinked. He thought, "Let me create worlds."

2.

He created these worlds: water, beams of light, death and the waters below. Water is there above the heavens. The heavens are its support. The beams of light are the intermediate space, death is the earth[2] and the worlds below are the waters below.

3.

He thought, "These then are the worlds. Now let me create guardians for the worlds." From the waters he drew forth and fashioned a person.

4.

He brooded over him. When he had been brooded upon, his mouth burst forth like an egg, and from the mouth burst forth speech (*vāk*), and from speech, fire (*agni*).

The nostrils burst forth, and from the nostrils, breath, and from breath, air (*vāyu*).

The eyes burst forth, and from the eyes, sight, and from sight, the sun (*āditya*).

The ears burst forth, and from the ears, hearing, and from hearing, the directions (*dish*).

The skin burst forth, and from the skin, hair, and from hair, the plants and trees.

The heart burst forth, and from the heart, the mind, and from the mind, the moon (*chandramā*).

The navel burst forth, and from the navel, the downward breath, and from the downward breath, death (*mṛityu*).

The generative organ was separated out, and from the generative organ, the seed, and from the seed, water (*āp*).

Second Khaṇda

1.

These deities thus created fell into this mighty ocean.[3] He [*Ātmā*] afflicted the person with hunger and thirst. They said to him, "Find us a dwelling where we can establish ourselves and eat food."

2.

He brought a cow for them. "This is surely not enough for us," they said.

He brought a horse for them. "This is surely not enough for us," they said.

3.

He brought a person for them. "Yes, well done," they said. Indeed a person is well formed.

"Enter, each of you, into your own dwellings," he said to them.

4.
Fire (*agni*) became speech and entered the mouth.
Air (*vāyu*) became breath and entered the nostrils.
The sun (*āditya*) became sight and entered the eyes.
The directions (*dish*) became hearing and entered the ears.

Plants and trees became hairs and entered the skin.
The moon became the mind and entered the heart.
Death became the downward breath and entered the navel.
Water became the seed and entered the generative organ.

5.
Hunger and thirst said to him, "Find a dwelling for us." He said to them, "I will give you a place among these deities and let you share with them." Therefore to whatever deity an offering is made, hunger and thirst share it with that deity.

Third Khaṇda

1.
He thought, "Here are the worlds and the guardians of the worlds. Then let me create food for them."

2.
He brooded over the waters. From the waters over which he brooded there emerged a form. The form that emerged was food.

3.
The food that was created turned back and tried to run away.

He tried to catch it with speech. He could not catch it with speech. Indeed, had he been able to catch it with speech, one would be satisfied merely by uttering the word *food*.

4.
He tried to catch it with the breath. He could not catch it with the breath. Indeed, had he been able to catch it with the breath, one would be satisfied merely by smelling food.

5.
He tried to catch it with sight. He could not catch it with sight. Indeed, had he been able to catch it with sight, one would be satisfied merely by looking at food.

6.
He tried to catch it with hearing. He could not catch it with hearing. Indeed, had he been able to catch it with hearing, one would be satisfied merely by hearing about food.

7.
He tried to catch it with the skin. He could not catch it with the skin. Indeed, had he been able to catch it with the skin, one would be satisfied merely by touching food.

8.
He tried to catch it with the mind. He could not catch it with the mind. Indeed, had he been able to catch it with the mind, one would be satisfied merely by thinking about food.

9.
He tried to catch it with the generative organ. He could not catch it with the generative organ. Indeed, had he been able to catch it with the generative organ, one would be satisfied merely by emitting food.[4]

10.
He tried to catch it with the downward breath.[5] He caught it. Thus the one that is the grasper of food is *Vāyu* (air), for *Vāyu* is surely the one that is living on food.

11.
He thought, "How is it possible that this can exist without me?"

He thought, "Which way shall I enter?"[6]

He thought, "If speaking is through speech, if breathing is through the breath (*prāṇa*), if seeing is through the eyes, if hearing is through the ears, if touching is through the skin, if thinking is through the mind, if breathing out is through the outward breath (*apāna*), if emission is through the generative organ, then who am I?"

12.
Opening up the crown of the head, he entered by this gate. This gate is known as the cleft (*vidṛiti*). It is a place of delight. He has three dwellings, three states of sleep: this dwelling, and this and this.[7]

13.
Once born, he surveyed the creatures and thought, "Is there anything here I might speak of as another?" He perceived this

very person to be the all-encompassing Brahman. "This (*idam*) I have seen," he thought.

14.
Therefore he is called Idaṁdra,[8] for Idaṁdra is indeed his name. Though being Idaṁdra, they obliquely call him Indra, for indeed the gods seem fond of the indirect. Indeed the gods seem fond of the indirect.[9]

Second Adhyāya

1.
In a person this one first becomes an embryo. That which is the semen is the vigor gathered from all his limbs. He holds the self within himself. When he casts the seed in a woman, then he fathers it. That is one's first birth.

2.
It becomes one with the woman, just as a limb that is her own. Therefore it does not harm her. She nurtures this self of his that has entered her womb.

3.
She, the nurturer, should be nurtured. The woman fosters that embryo. The man nurtures the child both before and after birth.[10] In nurturing the child before and after birth, he is nurturing his own self for the continuation of these worlds, for in this way the worlds continue. That is one's second birth.

4.
His child, this self of his, takes his place in the performance of virtuous deeds, while his other self, having done what had to be done, grows old and departs. Once he departs from here, he takes another birth. That is one's third birth.

5.
This has been said by the seer:[11]

While yet lying in the womb,
I knew all the births of these gods.
A hundred iron forts constrained me,
yet I burst forth swift as a falcon.

This Vāmadeva said even while lying in the womb.

6.
Knowing this and having separated from the body, he soared upward. Enjoying all desires in that world of heaven, he became immortal. Yes, he became immortal.

Third Adhyāya

1.
"Who is this that we worship as the Self? Which of these is the Self?"

"It is he by whom one sees, by whom one hears, by whom one smells odors, by whom one speaks words, by whom one distinguishes the sweet from the not sweet."

2.
It is this heart and this mind. It is awareness (*saṁgyāna*), perception (*āgyāna*), discernment (*vigyāna*), consciousness (*pragyāna*), intelligence, insight, fortitude, thought, reflection, liveliness, memory, resolve, purpose, vitality, desire, mastery—all these are just names for consciousness.

3.
This is Brahman. This is Indra. This is Prajāpati. This is all these gods and these five great elements—earth, air, space, water, light. It is [big] creatures and various small ones, creatures of one sort or another—those born of an egg, those born of a womb, those born from moisture and those born of earth: horses, cows, humans, elephants. It is all that breathes here, both walking and flying, and all that does not move.

All that is guided by consciousness, founded in consciousness. The world is guided by consciousness. Its foundation is consciousness. Consciousness is Brahman.[12]

4.
By this Self which is consciousness, he rose upward from this world, and having obtained all desires in that world of heaven, became immortal. Yes, he became immortal.

May my speech rest on my mind.
May my mind rest on speech.
O manifest one, be manifest to me.
May both mind and speech secure the Veda for me.
May all that I have heard not depart from me.

By this study I shall bring together day and night.

I will speak what is right.
I will speak what is true.
May that protect me.
May that protect the speaker.
May it protect me.
May it protect the speaker.
May it protect the speaker.
Oṁ shāntiḥ shāntiḥ shāntiḥ

Shvetāshvatara Upanishad[1]

That is full; this is full.
From fullness, fullness comes out.
Taking fullness from fullness,
what remains is fullness.

All good I should hear from the ears, O radiant beings.
All good I should see through the eyes, O revered ones.
May we, full of praise, with bodies firm of limb,
enjoy the span of life given us by God.

Let us be together.
Let us eat together.
Let us be vital together.
Let us be radiating truth,
radiating the light of life.
Never shall we denounce anyone,
never entertain negativity.
Oṁ shāntiḥ shāntiḥ shāntiḥ

First Adhyāya

1.

Those who discuss Brahman say:
What is the cause? Is it Brahman? Why were we born?
By what do we live? On what are we established?
O knowers of Brahman, governed by whom do we live
in our different conditions, fixed in pleasure and pain?

2.

Time, one's own nature, necessity, chance, the elements,
the womb, man—are these regarded as the cause?
Is it a combination of these? It is not, however,
  because there is the Self.
Even the Self is unable to be the cause of pleasure and pain.

3.

Those devoted to the yoga of meditation (*dhyāna yoga*) saw
the power of the divine itself hidden by its own qualities.
He is the one who governs over
all these causes, from time to the Self.

4.

We understand him as a wheel with one rim, three coverings,
sixteen ends, fifty spokes, twenty counterspokes and six sets of
eight. His one form is manifold, having three separate paths,
and one delusion (*moha*) with two causes.

5.
We meditate on him as a river with five courses,
from five sources, mighty and winding, whose waves are
the five vital breaths, whose first source is the fivefold
intellect, with five whirlpools, a flooded current of fivefold
misery, with fifty divisions and five branches.

6.
In the vast wheel of Brahman in which all things live and rest,
the swan, the self, flutters about,
thinking himself and the mover to be separate.
But when blessed by him, he attains immortality.

7.
This is sung as the highest Brahman. Within it is the triad.[2]
It is the foundation, the imperishable. The knowers
of Brahman realizing what is therein, become absorbed
in Brahman. Devoted to that, they are freed from rebirth.

8.
The Lord supports all this together—the perishable
and the imperishable, the manifest and the unmanifest.
And the self, without the Lord, is bound, because he is
the enjoyer. On knowing God, he is released from all fetters.

9.
There are two unborn: the knower and the nonknower,
the all-powerful and the powerless.
And there is another who is unborn, connecting
the enjoyer and the objects of enjoyment.
When one discovers the three to be the infinite Self,
universal in form and nonactive, that is Brahman.

10.
Matter is perishable. The Self is immortal and imperishable.
The one God rules over the perishable and the Self.
By meditating on him, by striving toward him and in the end,
by becoming one with his nature, the illusion of the world
vanishes.

11.
On knowing God, all fetters fall off. With suffering destroyed,
birth and death cease. By meditating on him, at the dissolution
of the body there arises a third state, universal lordship,
which is the state of oneness, where desires are fulfilled.

12.
That eternal should be known as dwelling only in the Self.
Truly, there is nothing beyond this to be known.
By knowing the enjoyer, the enjoyed and enjoyment,
all has been taught. This is the threefold Brahman.

13.
The form of fire is not perceived in wood, yet its essence still exists, and once more it may be kindled from its source through a stick. Like that, the Self may be kindled in the body through the sound *Om.* So it is with both cases.

14.
Having made one's body the lower fire-stick
and sound the upper fire-stick,
through daily kindling the flame of meditation,
one may see, as if hidden, the divine.

15.
As oil in sesame seeds, as butter in milk,
as water in rivers, as fire in wood,
so the Self is found within oneself
when one discovers it through truthfulness and self-control.

16.
The Self pervades all, as butter pervades milk.
Rooted in self-knowledge and in discipline,
it is Brahman, the supreme wisdom.
Yes, it is Brahman, the supreme wisdom.

Second Adhyāya

1\.
Savitṛi,[3] first uniting his mind
and thought with truth,
perceived the light of Agni
and brought it from the earth.

2\.
With mind united,
we are in the care
of the divine Savitṛi
for the strength to obtain heaven.

3\.
With mind joined to the gods,
who by thought rise up to heaven,
may Savitṛi impel them
to create a great light.

4\.
The inspired seers of great wisdom unite their minds
and perform sacred rites for the intelligent Savitṛi.
He alone, knowing clearly, directs the ceremonial functions.
Great indeed is the praise of the divine Savitṛi.

5\.
I repeat your ancient prayer with adoration.
Let my verse go forth by the path of the sun.

May they listen—all the sons of immortality
who have risen to the celestial regions.

6.
Where the fire is kindled,
where the wind is directed,
where the *soma* overflows—
there the mind is born.

7.
With Savitṛi as the inspirer,
one should delight in the ancient Brahman.
Make your source there,
and your reward will never be diminished.

8.
With body steady, with head, neck and chest erect,[4]
drawing the senses and mind into the heart,
the wise man should cross by the raft of Brahman
all the streams begetting fear.

9.
Settling the breath inside, with movements stilled,
let him breathe through his nose with soft breath.
Let the wise man attentively quiet his mind,
as he would a chariot yoked with wild horses.

10.
Let him practice yoga in a clean and level place,[5]
free from pebbles, fire and dust, beautiful to the eyes,

settled by the sound of water and the like,
in a sheltered retreat protected from the wind.

11.
Fog, smoke, sun, wind, fire,
fireflies, lightning, crystal, the moon—
such are the appearances during yoga
which precede the cognition of Brahman.

12.
When the fivefold quality of yoga is produced,
arising from earth, water, fire, air and space,
then there is no sickness, old age or death
for him who has cultured a body tempered by the fire of yoga.

13.
Lightness, good health, freedom from desire,
a bright complexion, a pleasant voice,
a sweet smell and easily passed excretions—
these, they say, are the first results of progress in yoga.

14.
As a mirror tarnished by dust
shines bright when it is cleaned,
so a person, having seen the nature of the Self,
becomes one, becomes free of sorrow, his purpose fulfilled.

15.
And when the man who is united, using the nature
of his own Self (*Ātmā*) like a lamp to illumine

the true nature of Brahman, unborn, steadfast,
cleansed of all objects, he is released from all fetters.

16.
He indeed is the God who pervades all regions.
He was born first, and yet he is within the womb.
He alone was born, he alone will be born.
He stands before everyone. He is the face in every direction.

17.
The God who is in fire, who is in water,
who has entered into every being,
who is in herbs, who is in trees—
glory to that God. Glory to him.

Third Adhyāya

1.
He who spreads the net is one, commanding with
sovereign power, reigning over all worlds with might.
Who arises and comes together—he alone is one.
Those who know him become immortal.

2.
Truly Rudra is one. There is no place for a second
who commands these worlds with sovereign powers.
He dwells within all persons. He creates all worlds,
protects them and withdraws them at the end of time.

3.
Eyes on every side, face on every side,
arms on every side, feet on every side,
that one God, fashioning heaven and earth
with his arms, with his wings, welds them together.

4.
Rudra, the great seer, the Lord of the universe,
who creates and sustains the gods,
who of old gave birth to the golden germ (*hiraṇyagarbha*)—
may he grant us clear understanding.

5.
O Rudra, benign of form,
not causing fear, not showing evil,
with your peaceful form
look down on us, O dweller on the mountain.

6.
O dweller on the mountain, make benign
the arrow you carry in your hand to shoot.
O protector of the mountain,
injure not man nor anything that moves.

7.
Beyond this is Brahman, the highest, the vast,
concealed in all creatures, each and every one,
who alone encompasses all that is—
knowing him, the Lord, men become immortal.

8.
I know this great Purusha,
lustrous as the sun, beyond darkness.
One crosses over death only by knowing him.
There is no other way by which to go.

9.
There is nothing higher than he, nothing different,
nothing greater, nothing smaller.
Rooted in his own splendor, he stands like a tree, alone.
By him, Purusha, the whole world is filled.

10.
That which is unsurpassed
is without form and without affliction.
Those who know this become immortal;
others go only to sorrow.[6]

11.
He who is the face, head and neck of all,
who lives in the secret cave[7] of every being,
who pervades all, he is the Lord,
present everywhere, beneficent.

12.
Purusha is indeed the great Lord,
who impels the mind
to reach that highest state of purity.
He is the master, the eternal light.

13.
No bigger than a thumb is Purusha, the inner Self,
ever seated in the heart of beings,
shaped by feeling, by insight, by thought—
those who know that become immortal.

14.
Purusha has a thousand heads,
a thousand eyes, a thousand feet.
Encompassing the earth on every side,
he stands ten fingers' breadth beyond.[8]

15.
In truth Purusha is all this world,
what has been and what will be.
He is the Lord of immortality,
he who grows through food.

16.
With hands and feet on every side,
eyes, heads and mouths on every side,
with ears on every side,
he stands, enveloping this whole universe.[9]

17.
Appearing to have the qualities
of all the senses, yet devoid of every sense,[10]
he is the Lord of all, the ruler,
the great refuge of all.

18.
Embodied in the city of nine gates,
the swan sports in the world outside,
master of the whole universe,
of all that moves and moves not.

19.
Moving swiftly without feet, grasping things without hands,[11]
seeing things without eyes, hearing without ears,
he knows what is to be known, yet no one knows of him.
They call him the foremost, the great Purusha.

20.
Smaller than the smallest, greater than the greatest[12]
is the Self, hidden in the secret place of a living being.
One sees him, the great Lord, who is uninvolved,
and through the grace of the Creator, becomes free from sorrow.

21.
I know this ageless, ancient Self of all,
all-pervading, present everywhere.
They declare him to be free from birth.
The knowers of Brahman declare him to be eternal.

Fourth Adhyāya

1.
He who is himself without form gives rise to countless forms
in the beginning. He wields his power in manifold ways
for his own hidden purpose and in the end gathers all back
into himself. May that one God grant us clear understanding.

2.
He is Agni, fire. He is Āditya, the sun.
He is Vāyu, the wind. He is Chandramā, the shining one.
He is Shukra, the pure. He is Brahman.
He is the waters and he is Prajāpati, the Lord of created beings.

3.
You are woman. You are man.
You are the youth and the maiden too.
You are the old man hobbling along with a staff.
Once born, you are the face turned in every direction.

4.
You are the dark blue butterfly.
You are the green parrot with red eyes.
You are the thundercloud, pregnant with lightning.
You are the seasons, you are the seas.
You are without beginning, present everywhere.
You, from whom all worlds are born.

5.
There is one unborn female[13]—red, white and black—
which gives birth to many creatures alike in form.
One unborn male lies at her side, delighting in her.
Another unborn male leaves her, his enjoyment fulfilled.

6.
Two beautiful birds, bound by friendship,
cleave to the same tree.
One enjoys the sweet fruit,
the other looks on without eating.[14]

7.
On the same tree a person, drowned [in ignorance],
suffers from want of power, completely bewildered.
When he sees the other, the adorable Lord,
and sees his greatness, he is freed from sorrow.[15]

8.
The verses of the Veda exist in the transcendental field,
which the *deva*s, responsible for the whole universe, inhabit.
He who is not open to this field, what can the verses
accomplish for him?
Those who know this are established in evenness.[16]

9.
The sacred meters and performances,
the rites and observances,
what was, what will be and what the Vedas proclaim—
all this the magician (*māyin*) sends forth.
The other[17] is ensnared in it by the magician's magic (*māyā*).

10.
One should know that the magic power (*māyā*)
is nature (*prakṛiti*), and the magician is the great Lord.
All this world is filled
with beings that are his parts.

11.
The one who presides over every birth,
in whom all this world comes together and spreads out,
the Lord, who bestows blessings, the adorable God—
by realizing him one gains transcendent peace.

12.
May Rudra, the great seer, the Lord of the universe,
who creates and sustains the gods,
who saw the birth of the golden germ (*hiraṇyagarbha*),
may he grant us clear understanding.

13.
Who is the Lord of the gods,
in whom the worlds find their rest,
who rules over two-footed and four-footed creatures—
to what God shall we offer oblations?[18]

14.
Subtler than subtle, in the midst of chaos
the creator of the world, endowed with many forms,
who alone encompasses all that is—knowing him,
the benign (*shiva*), one gains transcendent peace.

15.
Who at the right time protects the world, the Lord
of the universe concealed in all beings, in whom the seers
of Brahman and the deities find their union—
by thus knowing him, one cuts the fetters of death.

16.
By knowing the benign one, concealed in all beings
like the cream in clarified butter,
who alone encompasses all that is—
by knowing God, one is released from all fetters.

17.
That God, maker of all things, the great soul,
ever seated in the heart of beings,
he is shaped by the heart, the understanding, the mind.
They who know this become immortal.[19]

18.
When there is no darkness [of ignorance], there is neither
day nor night, neither being nor nonbeing, just the benign
one alone (*shiva eva kevala*)—that is the imperishable,
that is the splendor of Savitṛi,[20] and from that the ancient
wisdom sprang forth.

19.
Not from above, nor from across,
nor from the middle can he be caught.
He is beyond measure,
who is called most glorious.

20.
His form is not to be perceived.
No one sees him with the eyes.[21]
They become immortal who with heart and mind
know him as dwelling in the heart.

21.
"You are unborn," thinking thus,
someone approaches in fear.
"O Rudra, with your kindly face
protect me always.

22.
"Harm us not in our child or grandchild, harm us not
in our life,
harm us not in our cattle, harm us not
in our horses,
slay not our heroes in your anger, O Rudra.
We invoke you always with offerings."

Fifth Adhyāya

1.
There are two, knowledge and ignorance, which are lodged in the imperishable, infinite supreme Brahman where they lie hidden. Ignorance is perishable, knowledge is immortal. Yet he who rules over knowledge and ignorance is another.

2.
The one who presides over every birth,
over all forms and all wombs, is he who in the beginning
carries *hiraṇyagarbha*[22] in his thoughts
and witnesses that firstborn being born.

3.
Spreading out net after net in countless ways,
this God withdraws them into that field.[23]
Creating again and again by virtue of his powers
the Lord, the great soul, rules over all.

4.
As the sun shines, lighting up all regions,
above, below and across,
so that one God, glorious, most pleasing,
presides over all that is born of a womb.

5.
He is the womb of all, who matures his inherent nature
[into creation], who brings to full growth all that can grow,
who alone presides over this whole universe and is able
to apportion [to all things] their respective qualities.

6.
He lies hidden in the Upanishads, which are hidden
in the Veda. Brahmā knows him as the source of the Veda.
The *deva*s and *ṛishi*s of old knew him,
and becoming one with his nature, attained immortality.

7.
The person who, according to his tendencies, performs action
that bears fruit, surely experiences [the fruit of] that action.
Displaying various forms according to the three qualities,[24]
he, the king of life, wanders along the three paths according to
his own actions.[25]

8.
He is the size of a thumb, brilliant like the sun when
possessed of purpose (*saṁkalpa*) and sense of "I" (*ahaṁkāra*).
But when he has only the qualities of intellect and self,
he appears smaller than the point of an arrow.

9.
Know this living Self to be
a hundredth of a hundredth part
of the tip of a hair,
yet it partakes of infinity.

10.
This is neither male nor female,
nor is this neuter.
Whatever body it takes on,
with that it becomes identified.

11.
Deluded by imagination and the enticement of sight and touch, and by a wealth of food and drink, the self undergoes birth and aging. According to his deeds, the dweller in the body takes on form after form in different settings.

12.
The dweller in the body assumes many forms,
coarse and fine, based on his own tendencies,
as well as the tendencies of his past actions and his body.
The root cause of their union is seen to be yet another.[26]

13.
Without beginning, without end,
creator of the world from the midst of chaos,
of many forms, alone encompassing all that is—
on knowing God, one is released from all fetters.

14.
Those who know him who is attained by being him,[27]
who is said to be bodiless, the cause of existence and
nonexistence, who is benign, the author of creation
and its divisions,[28] they are liberated from their bodies.

Sixth Adhyāya

1.
Some learned men speak of inborn nature,
some of time. They are wholly deluded.
It is the great power of God in the world
by which this wheel of Brahman is made to turn.

2.
This whole world is ever pervaded by him who is the knower,
the creator of time, who understands all things and possesses
every attribute. Know that at his command, creation
appears as earth, water, fire, air and space.

3.
After performing this work [of creation]
and withdrawing again, he unites element with element,
by one, two, three or eight,
by time and inherent subtle tendencies (*guṇa*).[29]

4.
He starts the actions that are linked to the tendencies
and apportions all that is. When these have run
their course, what has been created is destroyed.
When the creation ceases, he goes on in essence as another.[30]

5.
The beginning, the source and cause of union, he is seen as
beyond past, present and future, without parts. That adorable

God of many forms is to be worshipped above all. He abides in one's own awareness, he who is the source of life.

6.
This world evolves from him, but he is other than the world tree,[31] beyond the play of time. Know him as dwelling in your own Self, immortal, the home of all that is, the bestower of *dharma*, the remover of evil, the Lord of prosperity.

7.
Him, the great Lord of lords, supreme, him, the supreme
deity of deities, him, the supreme ruler of rulers,
who transcends all—let us recognize him as God,
the Lord of the world, to be adored.

8.
For him there is nothing that has to be done.
His superior or even his equal is not seen.
His mighty power is revealed in infinite ways.
Intelligence, strength and activity are his by nature.

9.
No one in the world is his master.
No one rules over him. Of him there is no distinguishing sign.
He is the cause. He rules the rulers of the senses.
No one is father or mother to him.

10.
May the one God who by nature
covers himself like a spider

with threads produced from primal matter
grant us entry into Brahman.

11.
The one God hidden in all beings,
all-pervading, the inmost Self of all beings,
who oversees all actions, who dwells in all beings,
the witness, the one who is awake, alone, without qualities,

12.
the one who rules the motionless[32] many,
who makes manifold the single seed—
him the wise perceive seated in the Self.
To them, not to others, belongs happiness without end.

13.
He is the eternal of those eternal, the wakefulness of those awake, the one who fulfills the desires of many. Fathom that source through knowledge (*sāṁkhya*) and experience (*yoga*). On knowing God, one is released from all fetters.

14.
There the sun shines not, nor the moon nor stars,
nor do these lightnings shine, much less this fire.
Only when he shines does everything shine.
This whole world shines by his light.[33]

15.
He is the swan, alone amidst the world,
he is the fire lodged within the water.

Only by knowing him does one cross over death.
There is no other path by which to go.

16.
He is the maker of all, the knower of all, the self-born,
the perceiver, the maker of time, endowed with all attributes,
omniscient, the ruler of matter and spirit, the Lord
of nature's qualities, the cause of the cycle of existence—
of bondage, preservation and liberation.

17.
Absorbed in that, he is immortal.
He exists as the Lord, the perceiver, the omnipresent.
Protector of this world, he rules this world forever,
for none other is there to rule.

18.
Who creates Brahmā in the beginning,
who bestows the Vedas on him—
to that God, illuminated by his own intelligence,
do I, longing for liberation, go for refuge—

19.
to that God who has no parts, who is without activity,
tranquil, like a fire with its fuel spent,
who is beyond blame, spotless,
who is the surest bridge to immortality.

20.
Only when men shall roll up space
like a piece of leather
will there be an end to suffering
without knowledge of God.

21.
Through the power of meditation and through the grace of God the wise Shvetāshvatara realized Brahman and then truthfully proclaimed that knowledge as the highest means of purification, easy of access, to the advanced assembly of seers.

22.
The greatest secret contained in Vedānta,
which was proclaimed in a previous age,
should not be taught to anyone who is not at peace
or who is not one's son or student.

23.
To one who has the highest devotion for God,
and for the teacher as he has for God,
to that great soul the truths taught here are clearly revealed.
Yes, they are clearly revealed to that great soul.

That is full; this is full.
From fullness, fullness comes out.
Taking fullness from fullness,
what remains is fullness.

All good I should hear from the ears, O radiant beings.
All good I should see through the eyes, O revered ones.
May we, full of praise, with bodies firm of limb,
enjoy the span of life given us by God.

Let us be together.
Let us eat together.
Let us be vital together.
Let us be radiating truth,
radiating the light of life.
Never shall we denounce anyone,
never entertain negativity.
Oṁ shāntiḥ shāntiḥ shāntiḥ

Acknowledgments

We have been working on this translation, a labor of love, for several months each year, meeting in Italy, England and the USA. We would like to thank the many dear friends who generously offered food and lodging during this lengthy endeavor. Special thanks to Anthony Hardy for providing us with an ideal working environment during the final stages of the translation. In addition, we are grateful to Evan Finkelstein, Sue Brown, Sam Boothby, Leah Waller and Tom's wife, Linda, who offered thoughtful comments for the introduction. Judy Booth gave insightful suggestions for the text and the footnotes, and Fran Clark graciously did the initial proofreading. The group at Tarcher/Penguin have been encouraging and supportive, especially our editor, Mitch Horowitz. Dorian

Hastings used her eagle-eye vision to steer us through unforeseen complexities, and Balie Keown and Danielle Jackson offered immense help with the contract. Our heartfelt thanks go to all. This is their accomplishment as much as it is ours.

We would especially like to thank our own teachers: Vernon's advisor at Oxford University, Dr. S. Radhakrishnan, and Tom's advisor at the University of Virginia, Dr. K. L. Seshagiri Rao. Most of all, we are grateful to Maharishi Mahesh Yogi, who emphasized the role of experience as well as understanding for complete knowledge of the Upanishads. All that we have gained from the Upanishads is due to his guidance and teaching.

Endnotes

INTRODUCTION

1 Shankara's introduction to the Katha Upanishad. Shankara notes that the knowledge of Brahman must come from experience, not just from book learning.

2 Muktikā Upanishad 1.30–9.

3 According to sandhi rules, when "k" is followed by a voiced sound, it changes to "g." For example, Ṛik Saṁhitā, but Ṛig Veda. When no sound follows, it remains "k." For example, Ṛik.

4 According to sandhi rules, in this case when "s" is followed by a voiced sound, it changes to "r." For example, Yajur Veda. It remains Yajus if no sound follows or an unvoiced sound follows.

5 We have maintained the distinction between poetry and prose in the English translation, except in some cases.

6 We plan to publish the Bṛihadāraṇyaka, Chāndogya and Kaushītakī Upanishads in a future volume.

7 For the most part, we have followed the texts used by Shankara. In

interpreting the texts, we have also followed Shankara as much as we could. In addition, we have reviewed the translations of Hume (1921), Nikhilananda (1949), Radhakrishnan (1953), Gambirananda (1957), Olivelle (1996), and Roebuck (2000). We have used brackets [ ] in the translation when we have inserted words not in the original Sanskrit, but which we feel are essential for understanding.

8 Cited in Maurice Bloomfield, *The Religion of the Veda: The Ancient Religion of India (From Rig-Veda to Upanishads)* (New York and London: G. P. Putnam's Sons, 1908), 55.

9 Paul Deussen, *Outline of the Vedanta System of Philosophy according to Shankara* (New York: Grafton Press, 1906; Cornell University Library, 2009), "Preface."

10 Henry David Thoreau, *The Writings of Henry David Thoreau, Journal II: 1850–September 15, 1851* (Boston: Houghton Mifflin & Co., 1906), 4.

11 Ralph Waldo Emerson, *Journals and Miscellaneous Notebooks, Volume X: 1847–1848,* October 1, 1848 (Cambridge, Mass.: Belknap Press of Harvard University Press, 1973), 360.

12 Walt Whitman, *Leaves of Grass: The Original 1855 Edition* (Mineola, N.Y.: Dover Publications, 2007), 33.

13 Erwin Schrödinger, *My View of the World* (Woodbridge, Conn.: Ox Bow Press, 1983), ch. 4.

14 Niels Bohr, cited in Stephen Prothero, *God Is Not One: The Eight Rival Religions that Run the World* (New York: HarperOne, 2011), 144.

15 Cited in Sarvepalli Radhakrishnan, *The Principal Upaniṣads* (London: Allen & Unwin, 1953; New York: Harper, 1953), 940.

16 Ibid., 5–6.

17 We have used "Self" to denote unlimited, universal consciousness and "self" to denote limited, individual consciousness.

18 Bṛihadāraṇyaka Upanishad 1.4.10.

19 Katha Upanishad 2.3.17.

20 Muṇḍaka Upanishad 3.1.7–8.

21 Bṛihadāraṇyaka Upanishad 4.3.23, 26–28, 30.

22 Kena Upanishad 1.2.

23 *Ātmā* is the nominative of *Ātman*.

24 *Ātmā vāre drashtavyaḥ shrotavyo mantavyo nididhyāsitavyaḥ*, Bṛihadāraṇyaka Upanishad 2.4.5.

25 Muṇḍaka Upanishad 2.2.12.

26 Chāndogya Upanishad 3.14.1.

27 Māṇḍūkya Upanishad 2.

28 Īsha Upanishad 4–5.

29 A well-known verse describes *Purusha*, the cosmic spirit, as in this world and beyond this world: "Encompassing the earth on every side, he stands ten fingers' breadth beyond" (Ṛig Veda 10.90.1; Shvetāshvatara Upanishad 3.14).

30 Kena Upanishad 4.5.

31 Chāndogya Upanishad 6.11.

32 Bṛihadāraṇyaka Upanishad 1.4.10.

33 Māṇḍūkya Upanishad 2.

34 Aitareya Upanishad 3.1.3.

35 Taittirīya Upanishad 3.10.4.

36 Īsha Upanishad 16.

37 Kena Upanishad 1.4–8.

38 Muṇḍaka Upanishad 2.1.4.

39 Ibid., 2.2.5.

40 The acquisition of cattle was considered a sign of wealth.

41 Taittirīya Upanishad 3.6–9.

42 Muṇḍaka Upanishad 3.1.10.

43 Ibid., 2.1.1.

44 Katha Upanishad 1.2.16.

45 Ibid., 1.2.23.

46 Bṛihadāraṇyaka Upanishad 4.4.21.

47 Katha Upanishad 1.2.8.

48 Kena Upanishad 2.4.

49 Katha Upanishad 1.2.5, Muṇdaka Upanishad 1.2.8.

50 Katha Upanishad 1.2.9.

51 Ibid., 1.2.24.

52 Taittirīya Upanishad 2.4.1; 2.9.1.

53 Ibid., 2.7.

54 Ibid., 2.9.

55 Chāndogya Upanishad 7.1.3.

56 Katha Upanishad 1.2.22.

57 Taittirīya Upanishad 2.7.

58 Muṇdaka Upanishad 3.2.9.

59 Katha Upanishad 2.1.5.

60 Chāndogya Upanishad 6.1.4.

61 Radhakrishnan, *The Principal Upaniṣads*, 64.

62 Shvetāshvatara Upanishad 4.3–4.

63 A more general definition of an *āchārya* is one who is fully enlightened, knows the literature and engages in teaching.

64 Shankara, "Introduction" to the Īsha Upanishad, cited in Swami Nikhilananda, *The Upanishads: A New Translation, vol. 1* (New York: Bonanza Books, 1949), 197–198.

65 Ibid.

66 Īsha Upanishad 5.

67 Chāndogya Upanishad 6.2.1.

68 Brahma Sūtra Bhāshya 2.2.28, translated by K. V. Apte, *Brahma-Sūtra-Shankara-Bhāshya* (Bombay: Popular Book Depot, 1960), cited in Eliot Deutsch, *Advaita Vedānta: A Philosophical Reconstruction* (Honolulu: East-West Center Press, 1969), 31.

69 Shvetāshvatara Upanishad 1.6.

70 Katha Upanishad 2.1.11.

71 Muṇḍaka Upanishad 2.1.10.

72 Shankara, "Introduction" to the Īsha Upanishad, cited in Nikhilananda, *The Upanishads*, 199.

73 Chāndogya Upanishad 6.11. Each of the four *mahāvākya*s taught by Shankara is associated with one of the four seats of learning (*matha*) that he founded: "This Self is Brahman" (*ayam ātmā brahma*) is associated with the northern seat in Jyotirmath; "Consciousness is Brahman" (*pragyānaṁ brahma*) is associated with the eastern seat in Govardhana, near Puri; "I am totality" (*ahaṁ brahmāsmi*) is associated with the southern seat in Sringeri; and "Thou art that" (*tat tvam asi*) is associated with the western seat in Dvaraka.

74 Muṇḍaka Upanishad 3.2.9 (*brahmaveda brahmaiva bhavati*).

75 Deutsch, *Advaita Vedānta*, 9.

76 Swami Brahmānanda Saraswatī was addressed by Dr. Radhakrishnan as "Vedānta Incarnate."

77 Maharishi Mahesh Yogi, Seelisberg, Switzerland, June 1, 1973.

78 The Transcendental Meditation technique.

79 *Shāntaṁ shivam advaitaṁ chaturthaṁ manyante sa ātmā sa vigyeyaḥ*, Māṇḍūkya Upanishad 7.

80 Maharishi Mahesh Yogi, *Maharishi Mahesh Yogi on the Bhagavad-Gita: A New Translation and Commentary, Chapters 1–6* (New York: Penguin Books, 1990), 13.

81 Cited in Vernon Katz, *Conversations with Maharishi, vol.1* (Fairfield, Iowa: Maharishi University of Management Press, 2011), 283.

82 Ibid., 110.

83 *Shānti-pātha,* introductory verse, Īsha Upanishad. Each Upanishad begins and ends with an introductory and identical concluding verse, called *shānti-pātha* or *shānti-mantra.*

84 Maharishi Mahesh Yogi, *The Science of Being and Art of Living: Transcendental Meditation* (New York: Plume, 2001), 16.

85 *Ānandāddhyeva khalvimāni bhūtāni jāyante ānandena jātāni jīvanti ānandaṁ prayantyabhisaṁvishanti,* Taittirīya Upanishad 3.6.1.

86 Maharishi Mahesh Yogi, *The Science of Being and Art of Living,* 41.

87 Maharishi Mahesh Yogi, *Transcendental Meditation with Questions and Answers* (Fairfield, Iowa: Maharishi University of Management Press, 2011), 3.

88 Īsha Upanishad 6.

89 Shvetāshvatara Upanishad 6.21.

90 Ibid., 2.15.

ĪSHA UPANISHAD

1 *Īsha,* the first word of this Upanishad, means "Lord."

2 That unmanifest, this manifest.

3 The translation of this verse is by Maharishi Mahesh Yogi.

4 Shankara says in his commentary on this verse that since everything belongs to the Self, the desire for ownership is mistaken.

5 See Bṛihadāraṇyaka Upanishad 4.4.11.

6 *Tad dūre tad vantike.*

7 See Bhagavad-Gītā 6.29.

8 See Bṛihadāraṇyaka Upanishad 4.4.10.

9 The wholeness that is Brahman is more than either the ever-changing relative field of life or the nonchanging absolute field of life. "The

reality is eternity, immortality; so you taste immortality by virtue of being immortal. But to be immortal you have first to cross beyond the boundaries of change. Through change you can transcend change; through knowledge, that awakening, you taste immortality." Maharishi Mahesh Yogi, *Thirty Years Around the World: Dawn of the Age of Enlightenment, Volume One,* 1957–1964 (The Netherlands: MVU Press, 1986), 574.

10 *Hiraṇmayena pātrena satyasyāpihitaṁ mukham.*

11 This verse is addressed to the sun. Compare with Ṛig Veda 7.1.1. This verse brings out that the Self is everywhere, both near and in the furthest distance. See Īsha Upanishad verse 5.

12 See Bṛihadāraṇyaka Upanishad 5.15.1–4.

KENA UPANISHAD

1 *Kena,* the first word of this Upanishad, means "by whom," which addresses the central theme of the Upanishad. The Kena Upanishad is divided into four parts (*khaṇda*). The first two parts are mostly in verse and the last two are in prose.

2 The word is *deva,* which comes from the root *div,* "to shine." The usual translation is "god," but it also means "a being who shines," that is, God. God shines light upon and through material creation. The *devas* are the luminous intelligences that administer the various activities of the universe from the transcendental level of life.

3 See Īsha Upanishad 10 and 13.

4 There are different views about who is speaking. Shankara attributes this verse to the pupil.

5 See Muṇdaka Upanishad 3.2.4.

6 The word *pretya* is usually used in connection with "death," but Shankara interprets this word as signifying the attainment of the nondual state of awareness through identification with the Self.

7 *Agni* is "fire."

8 *Vāyu* is "the wind."

9 Shankara says that since *svarga* (heaven) is qualified by *ananta* (endless), it refers to Brahman.

KATHA UPANISHAD

1 Katha (Kaṭha) is the name of a sage and the founder of a branch of the Yajur Veda. The Katha Upanishad is composed of two chapters (*adhyāya*), each with three sections (*vallī*).

2 The translation of this verse is by Maharishi Mahesh Yogi. The first line, *saha nāvavatu,* is also translated, "May we both be protected." "Both" refers to the teacher and the student.

3 Nachiketas asks why he is being punished, since he is not the worst of the many sons or disciples around his father.

4 The general meaning of Yama, from the root *yam*, is "controller" or "ruler." Yama is the ruler of death, the administrator of death and immortality. Most of the verses in this Upanishad are ascribed to Yama.

5 Nachiketas is advising his father to keep his word, since all life is transitory.

6 Priest, highest of the four castes.

7 Yama is the son of Vivasvat.

8 Friendship (*saṁgatam*) is the result of association with holy people—Shankara.

9 True delight (*sūnṛitām*) is the fruit of sweet discourse—Shankara.

10 Auddālaki Āruṇi is the same person as Vājashravasa (verse 1) and Gautama (verse 10).

11 Death is not present in the heavenly world.

12 Because this *yagya* is named after Nachiketas, it is called the Nāchiketas fire.

13 Instruction by the mother, father and teacher; or instruction from scripture, either Shruti (revelation, what is heard) or Smṛiti (tradition, what is remembered), and the wise—Shankara.

14 Rituals, study of the Vedas and giving alms—Shankara.

15 Brahmā is the Creator, Brahman is universal wholeness, and Brāhmaṇa is a member of the priestly caste.

16 All this refers to Agni, the god of fire.

17 The third boon, which is about the nature of life after death.

18 See Muṇdaka Upanishad 1.2.8.

19 The Self is *Ātmā.*

20 A good teacher is needed to give the student the right direction, otherwise he or she may experience great difficulties.

21 The fruit of action.

22 The world of heaven, which is long-lasting, but not eternal—Shankara. It is also possible that the Upanishad is making the general point that the eternal has to be approached from the noneternal, which is a stepping-stone for the removal of ignorance, allowing the eternal to reveal itself. See also Katha Upanishad 1.3.2.

23 See Bhagavad-Gītā 2.20.

24 For the translation of verses 18 and 19, refer to Bhagavad-Gītā 2. 19–20, in Maharishi Mahesh Yogi, *On the Bhagavad-Gita,* 98–99.

25 See Shvetāshvatara Upanishad 3.20, *aṇoraṇīyān mahatomahīyān.*

26 See Īsha Upanishad 4–5.

27 The Self chooses itself. Self-effulgent, it shines by its own nature. As the sun reveals itself when the clouds disperse, so the Self reveals itself.

28 This verse is also found in Muṇdaka Upanishad 3.2.3. See also Bhagavad-Gītā 6.5.

29 The individual self and the universal Self.

30 The results of action done by oneself. Strictly speaking, the universal Self does not participate in the results of action, but because the two are found together, both are called enjoyers—Shankara.

31 According to Shankara, the highest place of Vishṇu is liberation.

32 The great self (*ātmā mahān*) is the golden embryo (*hiraṇyagarbha*), the

first manifestation. See Bhagavad-Gītā 3.42, which is similar, but not the same.

33 Primordial nature (*prakriti*), from which everything evolves, is like a swollen seed, ready to sprout.

34 The cosmic spirit is Purusha, the eternal silent witness, by virtue of which *prakriti* functions. Purusha can be easily found, since it is the inner Self. See Katha Upanishad 3.3.17.

35 The intellect.

36 The ultimate, the unchangeable Self.

37 Most translators have translated this line as "Seek out the boons." Shankara understands the word *varān* to mean "teachers."

38 This verse indicates the importance of following the teacher's instructions precisely.

39 See footnote to Katha Upanishad 1.3.10.

40 A ceremony in honor of the departed.

41 See Īsha Upanishad 6.

42 Verse 3, verses 5–9 and verses 12–13 end with "This indeed is that," indicating that the manifestations of Brahman mentioned there are nothing but Brahman.

43 See Ṛig Veda 1.154.

44 In the state of enlightenment, the experience of unity dominates the awareness to such an extent that one realizes that differences appear only on the surface, like waves on the ocean.

45 The body is described as having eleven gates: eyes, ears, nostrils, mouth, reproduction, evacuation, navel and crown of the head.

46 Set free in his lifetime, he does not take on another body.

47 For dwarf (*vāmana*), see Katha Upanishad 2.1.13, "the size of a thumb." Shankara interprets *vāmana* as "the adorable one."

48 Shankara mentions trees as something motionless.

49 See Muṇḍaka Upanishad 2.2.10 and Shvetāshvatara Upanishad 6.14; also Bhagavad-Gītā 15.6.

50 See Bhagavad-Gītā 15.1–3.

51 The root of the tree, according to Shankara. He calls it the highest state of Vishṇu.

52 The last lines are the same as Katha Upanishad 3.2.8.

53 According to Shankara, *prāṇa* stands for Brahman, which holds the universe in perfect order. As servants, fearing their master, follow his wishes, so does the universe follow the command of Brahman without a moment's respite.

54 See Taittirīya Upanishad 2.8.1.

55 Shankara equates the word *ātmā* with intellect here. When the intellect becomes clear as a mirror, then there arises a clear vision of Brahman (*brahma-vṛitti*).

56 In the other worlds, such as those of the fathers and *gandharvas*, the image of Brahman becomes less clear, while in the world of Brahmā it is distinct.

57 The verse emphasizes that the senses are separate in nature from the Self. Shankara says that each sense arises separately from one of the subtle elements. He compares their coming and going to waking and sleep states.

58 See Katha Upanishad 1.3.10, 11; also Bhagavad-Gītā 3.42.

59 Shankara says that he is realized by the understanding, or intellect, which is the ruler of the mind and resides in the heart.

60 See Shvetāshvatara Upanishad 4.20, 3.13 and 4.17.

61 Unqualified (*nirguṇa*) and qualified (*saguṇa*) Brahman. First *nirguṇa* Brahman is realized and then both are realized as one state: Brahman.

62 This verse is also found in Bṛihadāraṇyaka Upanishad 4.4.7.

63 This refers to different forms of embodiment. See Chāndogya Upanishad 8.6.6 and Prashna Upanishad 3.6.

PRASHNA UPANISHAD

1 The word *prashna* means "question." This Upanishad is composed of six questions.

2 Firewood is for the ritual ceremony done at the beginning of instruction. Carrying firewood indicates the student's readiness to be instructed by the teacher.

3 See Maitrī Upanishad 6.8.

4 This verse from the Ṛig Veda may refer to the sun coursing in the sky, forming a year with five seasons, twelve months, etc. The sun, who sees all, creates the clouds, which are rich in water. The following verses discuss the months and days of the month.

5 The rule spoken of in verse 13.

6 The word is *bāṇa,* which literally means "reed." The word also refers to the number five—the five senses.

7 Maghavan, a word denoting Indra, chief of the gods.

8 The last line can be illustrated in the story from the Pūraṇas about the churning of Mount Mandara at the beginning of creation. This required the force of both *devas* and *asuras*, being and nonbeing, consciousness and physiology—both are needed to create the nectar of immortality.

9 Ṛig Veda, Yajur Veda, Sāma Veda, *yagya* (Vedic performance), *kshatriya* (rulers) and *brāhmaṇa* (priests).

10 Shankara interprets "the seers" as the senses here.

11 Mātarishvan is Vāyu, the wind.

12 Eyes, ears, nostrils and mouth. According to Shankara, digestion supplies nourishment to these organs. Refer also to Muṇdaka Upanishad 1.2.4 and 2.1.8.

13 See Katha Upanishad 2.3.16.

14 See Prashna Upanishad 3.7 and 3.8.

15 Ibid., 3.1.

16 The body.

17 Refer to Muṇḍaka Upanishad 1.1.4.

18 In Sanskrit phonology, *o* is composed of *a* and *u.* Refer to Māṇḍūkya Upanishad 8–11.

19 Shankara identifies Brahmā with the totality of living beings.

20 In the waking, dreaming and sleeping states. The implication is that in all three states one is awake inside. See Māṇḍūkya Upanishad 8–11.

21 Sukeshā, the son of Bharadvāja, is known as Bhāradvāja.

22 See Prashna Upanishad 6.4.

23 According to Shankara, this refers to the four Vedas.

24 The worlds are the rewards of the rites.

25 Individuality.

MUṆDAKA UPANISHAD

1 *Muṇḍaka* means "shaved." According to tradition, everyone who hears this teaching is liberated from error. This Upanishad is traditionally for the *sannyāsī,* who has shaved his head and lives as a recluse. The Muṇḍaka Upanishad has three chapters (*muṇḍaka*), each with two sections (*khaṇḍa*).

2 Refer to Kena Upanishad 3.1.

3 Belonging to Agni and Soma, respectively.

4 A *devī* is a female deity.

5 See Bhagavad-Gītā 2.44.

6 It is not ritual itself that is frail. What is frail is ritual devoid of transcendental consciousness, *samādhi.* See Bhagavad-Gītā 2.42–44.

7 See Katha Upanishad 2.5.

8 Bhagavad-Gītā 8.18–21 uses the word *avyakta*, unmanifest, in a similar way—the unmanifest *prakṛiti* from which everything emerges and another aspect of the unmanifest, which is the ultimate reality.

9 The performances of Vedic rituals.

10 See Chāndogya Upanishad 5.10.

11 A *sādhya* is a celestial being.

12 Shankara refers everything in this passage to the senses, their perception and their objects.

13 "What is not" is understood by Shankara as what is subtle, formless, not apparent to the senses.

14 See Prashna Upanishad 3.4.

15 See Īsha Upanishad 15.

16 Refer to Katha Upanishad 2.2.15 and Shvetāshvatara Upanishad 6.14; also Bhagavad-Gītā 15.6.

17 See Ṛig Veda 1.164.20 and Shvetāshvatara Upanishad 4.6–7.

18 The national motto of India, inscribed on Indian currency, is *Satyam eva jayate,* "Truth alone triumphs."

19 See Īsha Upanishad 5.

20 Shankara notes that one is born amidst surroundings that have those objects of desire.

21 See Katha Upanishad 1.2.23.

22 See Bhagavad-Gītā 6.36 and Yoga Sūtras 1.14.

23 Shankara notes that there are two kinds of departure: Departure from the physical world and final departure from the bondage of ignorance. This verse refers to the latter.

24 See Prashna Upanishad 6.4.

25 Shankara refers *vigyānamaya-ātmā* to the self, which simulates the intellect in ignorance. In liberation, the Self and intellect are unmixed.

26 See Prashna Upanishad 6.4.

27 *Brahma veda brahmaiva bhavati.*

28 See Prashna Upanishad 2.11 and Īsha Upanishad 16.

29 According to Shankara, the head-vow (*shirovrata*) refers to carrying fire on the head, in preparation for a yagya and the instruction which follows. It could also refer to shaving the head (which denotes *muṇḍaka,* meaning *shaved*), a ritual for becoming a recluse.

MĀṆḌŪKYA UPANISHAD

1 *Māṇḍūkya* refers to *Māṇḍūka*, the name of the Vedic lineage descendant from Maṇḍu, a *ṛishi*. *Māṇḍūkya* also refers to *maṇḍūka*, a frog. In yoga, sitting still like a frog is called *maṇḍūkāsana*. Gauḍapāda, the teacher of Shankara, wrote a commentary on the Māṇḍūkya Upanishad, called the Māṇḍūkya Kārikā. The Māṇḍūkya Upanishad is the shortest of the Upanishads, with twelve verses.

2 This is one of the four great sayings (*mahāvākya*) of the Upanishads: *ayam ātmā brahma*.

3 Refer to Prashna Upanishad 5.3.

TAITTIRĪYA UPANISHAD

1 *Taittirīya* is the name for pupils of Tittiri, who founded a branch of the Kṛishṇa Yajur Veda. The story is told that his pupils gobbled up the text like partridges, hence the name *taitirīya*, which means "produced from a partridge" (*tittiri*). The Taittirīya Upanishad is divided into three parts (*vallī*), which are subdivided into sections (*anuvāka*).

2 The wind.

3 These utterances, known as *vyāhṛitis*, play a prominent role in Vedic ritual. They refer primarily to different planes of existence.

4 See Katha Upanishad, 2.1.12–13.

5 Shankara identifies Indra here with Brahman.

6 This whole passage appears to refer to the *sushumnā nādī*, the subtle vein which runs through the heart up to the top of the skull, where the soul finds liberation.

7 Each group contains five elements. See Bṛihadāraṇyaka Upanishad, where the idea is that realization of one group means all groups are realized.

8 *Om* is the primordial sound, considered sacred in India, which contains all other sounds and lies at the basis of all creation. It is traditionally used in the Vedic rituals.

9 Shankara says that Brahman here can refer to the Veda or to the supreme.

10 Shankara has teaching or reciting the Veda for *pravachanam.*

11 Speaker of truth.

12 Ever self-controlled.

13 The tree can be the *brahma-vṛiksha,* the tree of Brahman, or the *saṁsāra-vṛiksha,* the tree of the world, as described in Bhagavad-Gītā, 15.1–3. Shankara takes the second view—the tree of the cycle of life and death (*saṁsāra*) that needs to be uprooted.

14 Shankara makes much of the word *anu,* which means "upon" or "after." This is Trishanku's teaching after attaining knowledge, the Veda—that is, after having attained enlightenment.

15 Natural duty, natural law.

16 In the four stages of life (*āshrama*), the stage after study with the teacher is marriage and family life.

17 *Mātri-devo bhava pitri-devo bhava āchārya-devo bhava atithi-devo bhava.*

18 The word used here *is prashvasitavya,* which means "recovery of breath by means of a seat." A seat is given so that the teacher may recover his breath. Shankara also gives an alternative explanation, which is that there should be no stirring—not so much as a word should be breathed in the presence of the teacher.

19 Or according to one's means—Shankara.

20 Of the Veda.

21 To sons and pupils.

22 This is often translated as "body" or "trunk," but Shankara says that in the middle of the limbs, in the center of the body, is the self.

23 The parts of the body are compared to the limbs of a bird. This refers to the altar used for rites, which is in the shape of a bird, such as a falcon or a hawk. The tail of a bird brings stability in flight. See Maitrī Upanishad 6.33–34.

24 This refers to the Atharva Veda.

25 *Yato vācho nivartante.*

26 See 1.5.1–4. According to Shankara, this refers to the firstborn of creation.

27 Shankara also interprets the word *santam* (real) as "right path," meaning that knowledge contributes toward unfolding experience.

28 *Tat sṛishtvā tad evānupravishat.*

29 Shankara says that *real* here refers to "relative, empirical reality."

30 Shankara says that *real* here refers to "Brahman."

31 Shankara refers to space (*ākāsha*) as the space within the heart.

32 See Bṛihadāraṇyaka Upanishad 1.4.2, "Certainly fear is born of duality" (*dvitīyād vai bhayaṁ bhavati*).

33 See Katha Upanishad 2.3.3.

34 Compare with Bṛihadāraṇyaka Upanishad 4.3.33.

35 Higher beings, who make music, are called *gandharvas.*

36 Who is a knower of the ultimate reality on the level of experience and understanding.

37 See Īsha Upanishad 16.

38 The word here is *tapas,* which means "going within," but is usually translated as "austerity." "Austerity means denial of the pleasures of the senses, or coming out of the field of sensory activity and enjoyment. The purpose of austerity is to purify by freeing the mind from the impact of the objects of sense." Maharishi Mahesh Yogi, *On the Bhagavad-Gita,* 166.

39 *Ānandāddhyeva khalvimāni bhūtāni jāyante ānandena jātāni jīvanti ānandaṁ prayantyabhisaṁvishanti.*

40 According to Shankara, this means he is able to properly assimilate food.

41 Note that the Upanishad shows that when one is established in the transcendental state, one's desires are automatically fulfilled. It is not that such passages are later additions or are unworthy of the Upanishads—they are an integral part of the teaching.

AITAREYA UPANISHAD

1 The Aitareya Upanishad was said to be cognized by Mahidāsa Aitareya. It is in three parts (*adhyāya*), with the first part divided into three sections (*khaṇda*).

2 The earth is called death because life on earth ends in death.

3 The ocean of mundane existence.

4 The essence of food is semen.

5 The downward breath (*apāna*) is the downward movement of digestion, which assimilates vital energy from food.

6 Shankara says that one can enter either through the tip of the foot or the crown of the head.

7 Compared to the fourth state of consciousness (*turīya*), waking, dreaming and deep sleep are all as good as sleep.

8 Perceiver (*dra*) of this (*idam*).

9 See Bṛihadāraṇyaka Upanishad 4.2.2.

10 Through performance of the requisite ceremonies.

11 See Ṛig Veda 4.27.1.

12 *Pragyānaṁ brahma.*

SHVETĀSHVATARA UPANISHAD

1 The Shvetāshvatara Upanishad is named after the sage Shvetāshvatara, "he who has a white (*shveta*) horse (*ashva*)" or "he whose senses (*ashva*) are pure (*shveta*)." Shvetāshvatara, the main teacher in the Upanishad, is said to have imparted the Upanishad to a group of advanced disciples. The Upanishads is divided into six chapters (*adhyāya*).

2 According to Shankara, the *triad* is the individual soul, the world and the universal soul.

3 *Savitri* is the sun.

4 See Bhagavad-Gītā 6.13.

5 Ibid., 6.11.

6 See Bṛihadāraṇyaka Upanishad 4.4.14.

7 The cave of the heart.

8 This and the following verse are the same as Ṛig Veda 10.90.1 and 10.90.2.

9 See Bhagavad-Gītā 13.13.

10 These two lines are the same as Bhagavad-Gītā 13.14.

11 See Īsha Upanishad 5.

12 See Katha Upanishad 1.2.20.

13 The Sanskrit word *ajā* can mean both "unborn female" or "nanny goat." The unborn female is *prakṛiti* (nature), whose three constituent qualities are white (*sattva*), red (*rajas*) and black (*tamas*). The three qualities are the three *guṇas*: *sattva* (purity), *rajas* (energy) and *tamas* (dullness). The unborn male is Purusha, who is subject to bondage and who leaves her upon liberation.

14 See Ṛig Veda 1.164.20 and Muṇdaka Upanishad 3.1.1.

15 See Muṇdaka Upanishad 3.1.2.

16 See Ṛig Veda 1.164.39.

17 The individual soul.

18 See Ṛig Veda 10.121.3.

19 See Katha Upanishad 2.3.9.

20 This is the first line of the *gayatrī mantra—tat savitur vareṇyam.*

21 See Katha Upanishad 2.3.9.

22 The golden germ is *hiraṇyagarbha*, the first of created entities.

23 The field refers to primal nature, parā prakṛiti, the source of creation.

24 See Shvetāshvatara Upanishad 4.5.

25 The three paths according to Shankara are *dharma* (path according to natural law), *adharma* (path not in accord with natural law) and *gyāna* (path of knowledge); or alternatively *devayāna* (path of the gods), *pitṛiyāṇa* (path of the ancestors) and *manushyayāṇa* (path of mankind).

26 The word "another" refers to God, the subject of the next verse.

27 Rather than through external means.

28 For the divisions, see Prashna Upanishad 6.4.

29 The one is Purusha; the two, *Purusha* and *prakṛiti*; the three, the three *guṇas*; the eight, the eightfold *aparā prakriti*, which is manifest. See Bhagavad-Gītā 7.4. The idea here is that God brings about the union of spirit and matter by means of creation.

30 When the three *guṇas* lose their equilibrium, creation begins, and when they regain their equilibrium, creation dissolves. Still the Creator goes on.

31 See Katha Upanishad 3.3.1; also Bhagavad-Gītā 15.1–3.

32 Attributing activity solely to matter is an illusion because matter independent of consciousness is inert.

33 See Muṇḍaka Upanishad 2.2.10 and Katha Upanishad 2.2.15; also Bhagavad-Gītā 15.6.

About the Translators

Vernon Katz received his doctorate from Oxford University, where he studied the Upanishads with Sarvepalli Radhakrishnan, who later became president of India. Katz later assisted Maharishi Mahesh Yogi, the founder of Transcendental Meditation, in his classic translation of the Bhagavad-Gītā (Penguin, 1969) and the Brahma Sūtras. Katz has written three additional books: *Conversations with Maharishi: Volume I; Conversations with Maharishi: Volume II;* and *The Blue Salon and Other Follies*, an account of growing up as a Jewish boy in Nazi Germany. Katz is a trustee emeritus and visiting professor at Maharishi University of Management in Fairfield, Iowa. He lives in England.

Thomas Egenes received his doctorate from the University of Virginia, after graduating from the University of Notre Dame. He is an associate professor at Maharishi University of Management and the author of one Sanskrit translation (*Maharishi Patañjali Yoga Sūtra*) and five other books: *Introduction to Sanskrit: Part One; Introduction to Sanskrit: Part Two; Learning the Sanskrit Alphabet; All Love Flows to the Self*; and *Eternal Stories from the Upanishads*, a retelling that includes selections of direct translations. His popular guides for learning Sanskrit are used at universities in the United States, Europe and Australia. He lives in Fairfield, Iowa.